T0198565

THE EVERYTHING KIDS'

MUMMIES, PHARAOHS, AND PYRAMIDS

PUZZLE AND ACTIVITY BOOK

DISCOVER THE MYSTERIOUS SECRETS OF ANCIENT EGYPT

Beth L. Blair and Jennifer A. Ericsson

Adams Media
New York   London   Toronto   Sydney   New Delhi

Adams Media
An Imprint of Simon & Schuster, Inc.
57 Littlefield Street
Avon, Massachusetts 02322

An Everything® Series Book.
Everything® and everything.com® are registered trademarks of Simon & Schuster, Inc.

ADAMS MEDIA and colophon are trademarks of Simon and Schuster.

For information about special discounts for bulk purchases, please contact Simon & Schuster Special Sales at 1-866-506-1949 or business@simonandschuster.com.

The Simon & Schuster Speakers Bureau can bring authors to your live event. For more information or to book an event contact the Simon & Schuster Speakers Bureau at 1-866-248-3049 or visit our website at www.simonspeakers.com.

Interior illustrations by Kurt Dolber.
Puzzles by Beth L. Blair.

Manufactured in the United States of America

10 9 8 7 6 5 4 3 2
March 2017

ISBN 978-1-59869-797-1

CONTENTS

INTRODUCTION

A Long, Long Time Ago . . .

What was it like to live in ancient Egypt? Pharaohs were the kings of the day, hundreds of gods and goddesses controlled your daily life, the pyramids were just being built, and (if you were rich enough) you got to be turned into a mummy!

Even though this period of time started more than 4,000 years ago, people continue to be fascinated by its beauty and mystery. *The Everything® Kids' Mummies, Pharaohs, and Pyramids Puzzle and Activity Book* is full of fun facts and crazy jokes that will bring you back to the time of the pharaohs. There are word searches, mazes, acrostics, codes, picture puzzles, and much more. Want something different? Try making your own mummy, creating mini-pyramids, or writing in hieroglyphs. Itching to explore? Crawl through a pyramid or peer inside a mummy while you learn about the high-tech ways that ancient Egypt is still being studied today!

To give you a taste of some of the treasures in store, we're going to send you off on an archaeological dig. On the next page, you will find outlines of things that were important in ancient Egyptian life. See how many of each of them you can excavate, or uncover. Write the number in the space below the outline. Check the answer key in the back of the book to see if you were right. Then dig in and enjoy the rest of our "puzzling" journey into ancient Egypt!

Beth L. Blair

Jennifer A. Ericsson

Look for me and my buddy all through the book!

We know a lot about ancient Egypt!

Scarab Beetle **Pyramid** **The Sun** **Nile River**

HINT: Highlight each shape with a different color as you count them!

v

CHAPTER 1

WHAT IS A MUMMY?

Death Decay

After death, a body starts to break down or rot. Microscopic plants and animals such as bacteria and fungi feed on the corpse until soft tissues like skin, muscles, and organs are gone! Only bones are left.

Finish these words that contain the letters R-O-T.

Orange vegetable = _ _ _ R O T

Thin soup = _ R O T _

A slow run = _ R O T

Turn around = R O T _ _ _

Colorful bird = _ _ _ R O T

Past tense of write = _ R O T _

Opposite of sister = _ R O T _ _ _

Keep from harm = _ R O T _ _ _

Why Not Rot?

Fill in the missing vowels to find out!

Why d_dn't _gypt__n m_mm__s r_t?

Th_ _gypt__ns w_rk_d h_rd t_ m_ke s_r_ th_t w_ d_d n_t!

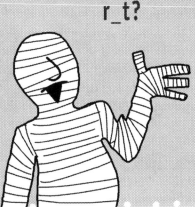

2

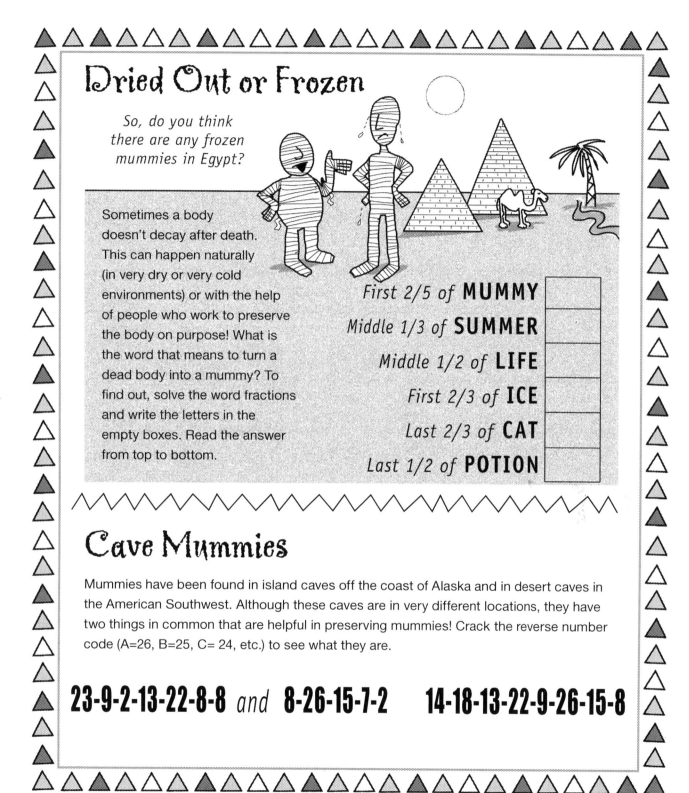

Dried Out or Frozen

So, do you think there are any frozen mummies in Egypt?

Sometimes a body doesn't decay after death. This can happen naturally (in very dry or very cold environments) or with the help of people who work to preserve the body on purpose! What is the word that means to turn a dead body into a mummy? To find out, solve the word fractions and write the letters in the empty boxes. Read the answer from top to bottom.

First 2/5 of **MUMMY**

Middle 1/3 of **SUMMER**

Middle 1/2 of **LIFE**

First 2/3 of **ICE**

Last 2/3 of **CAT**

Last 1/2 of **POTION**

Cave Mummies

Mummies have been found in island caves off the coast of Alaska and in desert caves in the American Southwest. Although these caves are in very different locations, they have two things in common that are helpful in preserving mummies! Crack the reverse number code (A=26, B=25, C= 24, etc.) to see what they are.

23-9-2-13-22-8-8 *and* 8-26-15-7-2   14-18-13-22-9-26-15-8

Water, Water

To make a mummy, all of the water trapped in the cells of the body must be removed as quickly as possible. But an adult human body contains a lot of water! How much? You do the math to add and subtract these glasses of water.

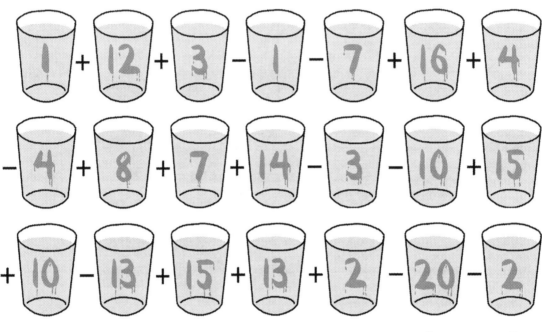

$$1 + 12 + 3 - 1 - 7 + 16 + 4$$

$$- 4 + 8 + 7 + 14 - 3 - 10 + 15$$

$$+ 10 - 13 + 15 + 13 + 2 - 20 - 2$$

No, wait!!!

An adult human body is ☐% water.

All Sorts of Mummies

Mummies can be made in many different ways, but all mummies fall into two categories. If you had a big pile of mummies, how would you sort them? Find the two "extra" capital letters in each statement below. Put the first one in the space to the left of the statement. Put the second one in the space to the right of the statement. After you have collected all the letters, read them from top to bottom.

The suN and warM winds can dry out a corpse.

Extreme cold will freeze And preserve A body.

SomeTimes organs were removed, dried, aNd replaced.

MoistUre can be reMoved from a body using salt.

FiRe and smoke Are both good drying methods.

An Acidic, wet environment prevents Decay.

ChemicaLs can also be used to preserve thE body.

What kind of mummies do you think we are?

Hmmm...

A World of Mummies

Egypt isn't the only country where mummies were made. Mummies have been discovered in many places across the globe, including the countries listed here. See if you can fit all these names into the puzzle grid. We left a P-L-A-N-E to help you travel around the world!

Hello!

¡Hola!

Argentina, Austria, Canada, Chile, China, England, Germany, Greenland, Holland, Italy, Jordan, Mexico, Peru, USA

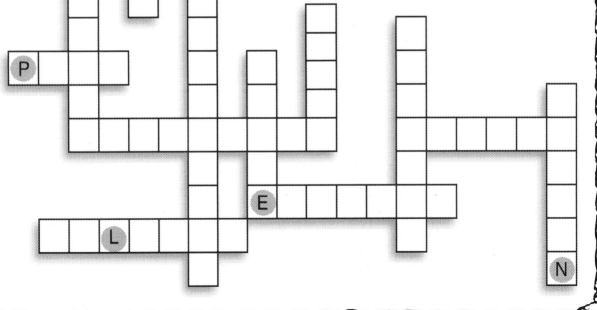

The Oldest Mummies

Egyptian mummies may be the most famous, but the Egyptians were not the first mummy makers. The oldest human-made mummies have been found on the coast of Chile, in South America. The Chinchorro people were making mummies 2,000 years before the Egyptians! Here are the directions for how the Chinchorro made their mummies. Number the boxes so that the steps are in the correct order.

Then remove all of the organs.	Finally, add a mask and wig.	Place the skin back on top of the paste.
Paint the replaced skin with special minerals that turn black.	Cover stuffed body with white paste made from ashes.	First, take all the skin off of the mummy-to-be.
Stuff the empty body with clay, straw, fur, etc.		

How do you think we were made??

That sounds awful!

7

Going Up!

The native Chachapoyas of Peru hid their mummies high on cliffs that jutted out of the jungle. The Chachapoyas were very smart because down lower where they lived it was cool, wet, and rainy. High above the treetops the cliffs were warm and dry—perfect for mummies! START at the bottom of the cliff and climb until you can enter the tomb.

START

Bog Bodies

In northern Europe and the British Isles, many mummies have been pulled from swamps or bogs. Natural chemicals in the water accidentally turn these bodies into mummies. Sadly, people did not end up in the bogs by accident—most of these mummies show signs of force and violence! Scientists believe three kinds of victims were put in the bogs. For each puzzle below, two words have been placed on top of the other. Figure out the pattern that will help you separate the words and learn what kind of people these were.

1. CCORMIMMOINNALS

2. PHHAYNSDIICCAALPLPYED

3. HSUAMCARNIFICE

Now you're going to have to get all rewrapped!

HELP!!

Yummy?

Some bog bodies are so well preserved that scientists can tell a very interesting thing about them. What is it? Break the vowel switch code to find out!

WHOT THU MIMMAUS LOST OTU!

What's Inside?

The Inca people of South America often placed their dead in a sitting position and wrapped them tightly with cord. The body was then packed with layers of fabric and offerings such as food, feathers, and shells. By the time everything was packed, wrapped, and tied, you couldn't really tell there was a human inside! To find the common name for this ancient surprise package, cross out all the letters W-R-A-P. Read the remaining letters from top to bottom and left to right.

Is any body home?

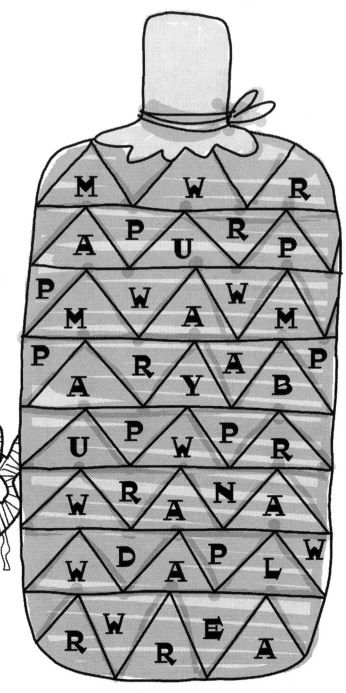

10

Many Mummies

One type of mummy is the most numerous—the count is estimated to be in the millions! Use the clues to fill in the clay pots. The last letter of one word is the first letter of the next. When you have finished, read the letters from the dark pots.

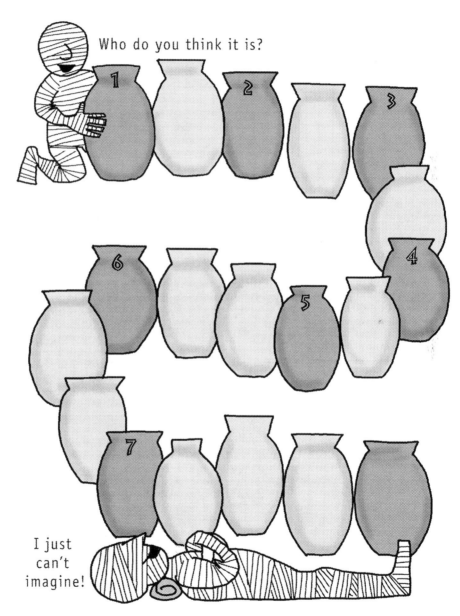

Who do you think it is?

1. What a chicken lays

2. Opposite of gal

3. Little dog noise

4. Round cooking object

5. Rented ride

6. A thought

7. Nut of an oak tree

I just can't imagine!

Planning Ahead

In Japan, some Buddhist priests tried to start the mummification process while they were still alive! They would go on an extreme diet, drink a special toxic tea, and finally sit motionless in a small tomb. This process was not quick! To find out how long these priests would work at becoming mummies, figure out where to put the letters in each column of this puzzle. The letters all fit in the boxes under their own columns.

I'm bored. How long until we turn into mummies?

A	O	O				Ø	N				H	R			
T	B	E		T	Ø	D	T		T	S	Ā	O	A		
A	H	D	U	P	I	T	C	N	R	I	E	O	T	O	K
W	N	R	K	D	R	U	E	E	S	Y	A	T	W	S	K	Y	S

						O			S				O		
	B			■					■			A			■
			■					■	'		■		W		
W			■	O				■			G			!	

CHAPTER 2

FAMOUS PHARAOHS

What's in a Name?

The pharaohs were the rulers, or kings, of ancient Egypt. But the word "pharaoh" did not always mean a person. Finish this puzzle to learn what it originally meant! Each of the clues suggests a word. Write the word on the dotted lines, then transfer each letter into the numbered grid.

1A	2A	3B		
4B	5B	6C	7B	8C
9C	10A	11B	12C	13C

A. Opposite of cold

$\overline{}$ $\overline{}$ $\overline{}$
2   10   1

B. To fight with loud words

$\overline{}$ $\overline{}$ $\overline{}$ $\overline{}$ $\overline{}$
7   5   4   11   3

C. Bed linen used as a ghost costume

$\overline{}$ $\overline{}$ $\overline{}$ $\overline{}$ $\overline{}$
12   9   6   13   8

Only One

Pharaohs ruled one at a time, and power passed down through the family, usually from father to son. Find the one time "pharaoh" is spelled correctly and fill in the bubble letters.

Remember, words in the grid can be spelled backwards or from bottom to top!

H P H A H R
A H P H O R
R O H A A P
O R A O R H
H A R R A A
O R A A H R
P H A R P O
H O H P H A
A R O O P H

14

Link to the Gods

A pharaoh was not only a king, he was also the most important religious leader in the country. The Egyptian people saw the pharaoh as the link between themselves and the gods. What else did they believe the pharaoh to be? To find out, look at these pairs of bracelets. Some look like they are linked through each other. Others look like they overlap but are not linked. Use a light color marker to circle the pairs of bracelets that are linked. Read the letters in them from left to right and top to bottom.

SC AR   TH EY   YF AC   ES WE

BE LI   RE CA   EV ED   TH EP

RV ED   HA RA   IN TO   OH WA

TU RN   SA LI   EE TS   VI NG

OR PO   GO D!   TA TO   ES ON

D Is for Divine

Ancient Egyptians had a passion for cleanliness. That's why most men were clean-shaven, with no hair on their faces. However, a beard was thought to be a divine characteristic of an Egyptian god. If a beardless pharaoh wanted to show that he was also a god, what would he do? To find out, circle all the words that do not rhyme with HAIR. Start by the pharaoh's ear and read the circled words around the border.

EXTRA FUN:
Color the pharaoh's blue and gold striped headdress, called the "Nemes Crown."

Help this pharaoh be divinely dressed. Connect the four dots and color in his you-know-what!

BARE BEARD THERE HELD SHARE ONTO MARE

LAIR FAKE STAIR PAIR A WEAR WORE AIR HE

HIS STARE CARE CHIN BEAR SNARE WITH DARE PEAR A RARE

CORD

Girls Rule!

Most pharaohs were men, but there were a few women rulers. Queen Hatshepsut was supposed to rule in her son's name until he grew up, but she began to call herself pharaoh and made her own laws! Statues of Hatshepsut often show her dressed like a king and wearing something that only male pharaohs wore. What was it? Use the decoder to find out!

/O⌐ ⋂O⋂⌐

⋀ ⌐⋀⌐/⌐

⌐⌐⋀⋁⊃

A	⋀	K	<
B	⌐	L	⌐
D	⊃	O	O
E	⌐	R	\
F	⌐	S	/
H	⊙	W	⋀

How Do I Look?

Today Queen Hatshepsut is dressed for a party and is checking her royal reflection in a mirror. But something is not right! Can you find the eight differences between the two images?

On Top

A pharaoh's crown looked different depending on when and where he ruled. Here are five of the different crowns of ancient Egypt. Decide which one you like best and draw it on the pharaoh's head. Use the grid lines to help make the crown the correct size!

EXTRA FUN: Color the pharaoh's portrait when you are done.

The Nemes Crown is actually more like a headdress because it was made out of blue and gold striped fabric. The other crowns were probably made of painted leather.

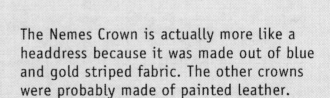

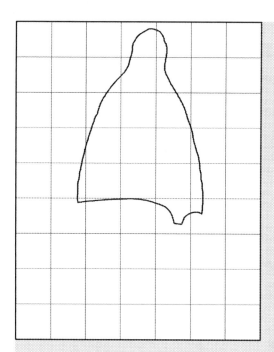

The White Crown was the symbol of Upper Egypt.

The Red Crown was the symbol of Lower Egypt.

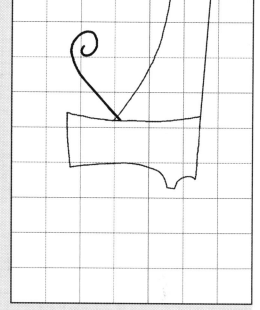

 **EXTRA FUN: You will need a piece of heavy paper or thin cardboard that is 14 inches wide and 18 inches long. Draw a grid pattern on it, making each square two inches. Copy your picture of the pharaoh onto the grid and color it in. Cut the picture apart on the grid lines to make a jigsaw puzzle!**

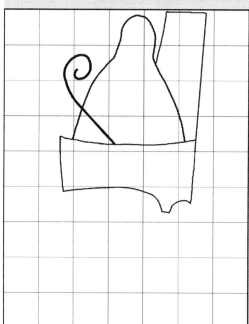

The Double Crown was the symbol of Upper and Lower Egypt together. Guess what colors it was!

The Blue Crown was also called the War Crown.

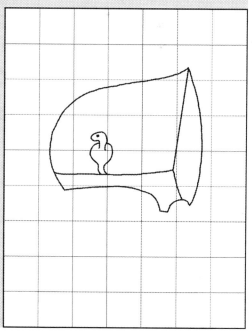

19

King Tut

King Tutankhamun is probably the most famous pharaoh, but he was not a powerful ruler. This is because he became king at about age nine, and other adults were really in charge. Because of his young age, historians often refer to Tut by a nickname. To find out what it is, put these words in alphabetical order and read the shaded letters from top to bottom.

FAKE

CAB

HID

BATH

DUTY

JUG

HINT

BED

DOOR

ATE

1.

2.

3.

4.

5.

6.

7.

8.

9.

10.

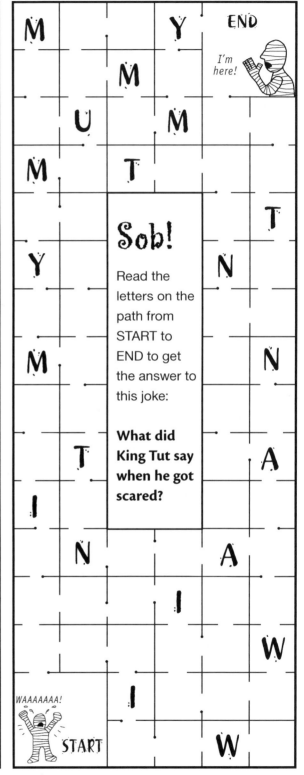

Sob!

Read the letters on the path from START to END to get the answer to this joke:

What did King Tut say when he got scared?

I'm here!

END

START

WAAAAAAA!

Pha-ha-ha-raoh

Put each numbered letter on the correct line.

Where do pharaohs go out to eat?

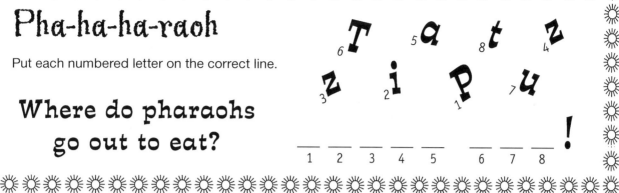

$$\underbrace{\quad}_{1}\ \underbrace{\quad}_{2}\ \underbrace{\quad}_{3}\ \underbrace{\quad}_{4}\ \underbrace{\quad}_{5}\quad \underbrace{\quad}_{6}\ \underbrace{\quad}_{7}\ \underbrace{\quad}_{8}\ !$$

Drama Queen

This famous queen of ancient Egypt led such a dramatic life that there are at least ten different Hollywood and TV movies about her! One story is that she was forced to flee Egypt during a political dispute. When she was ordered to return and face an angry military leader, the queen feared for her life. Thinking quickly, she had herself smuggled into the country rolled up in a rug! Who is this larger-than-life pharaoh? Break the minus-two-letter code to learn her name.

Hey, I can't breathe! I'm wrapped too tightly!

Yeah, I know about that!

21

Good King at Giza

Pharaohs were supposed to be fair and just, but many were tyrants! Of the three kings that had pyramids built at Giza, only one was considered to be especially honorable. Use the clues to help you cross out pyramids and find which one belongs to the good pharaoh buried at Giza.

▲ **The good pharaoh is not buried in the Great Pyramid.**

▲ **The smallest pyramid was not built at Giza.**

▲ **King Djoser built his pyramid at Saqqara.**

▲ **The good pharaoh is buried in the smaller of the remaining pyramids.**

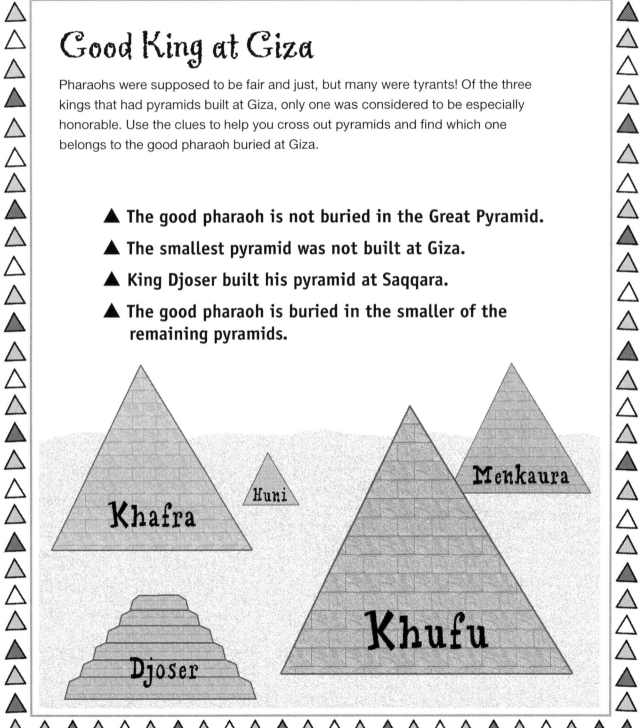

22

What a Great Guy!

This man was the greatest pharaoh that ever ruled Egypt. He was not only a strong military leader, he built more monuments and statues than any other pharaoh! To learn his name, place the letters in order on the dotted lines. Extra Fun: To see how long this pharaoh ruled, add together all the numbers inside the statues. Watch out for minus numbers!

King _ _ _ _ _ _ the second ruled for _ _ years.

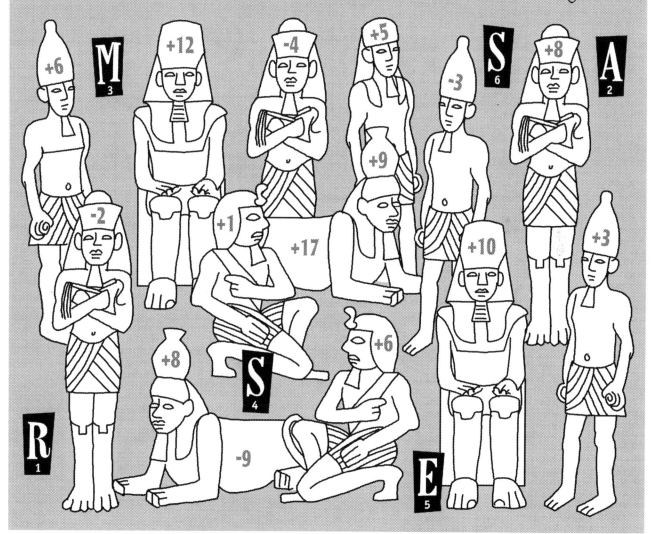

23

Shaking Things Up

During King Akhenaten's reign, he banished all traditional Egyptian gods—except for one! Cross out all the words with the letters A, B, or V. Read the remaining words from top to bottom to see who was the only god you could worship while King Akhenaten was in charge.

FAR	HAS	BET	YOU	AN
CAN	MAY	COULD	SHALL	BILL
EVERY	ONLY	ALL	EACH	THAT
LOVED	BIND	HATED	BOLD	WORSHIP
THE	BONE	BIT	THAT	BE
RAIN	BREEZE	SEA	SUN	FIVE
MAN	GOD	DEVIL	WOMAN	BABY

CHAPTER 3

LAND OF MANY GODS

Many Choices

Ancient Egyptians worshipped a lot of different gods and goddesses. They believed that each one had a role to play in keeping harmony in the world. The main gods had important jobs like directing the sun, the weather, and the afterlife. Lesser gods had smaller jobs, like protecting people from spider bites! Color in all the boxes that have a horizontal line to see approximately how many gods it took to keep things running smoothly.

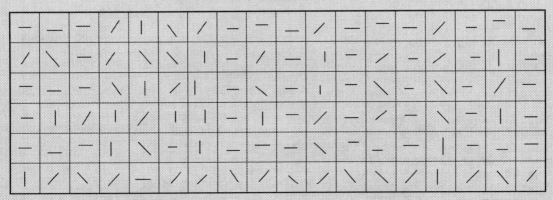

Who Are You?

Trying to keep all the god and goddesses straight is quite confusing. Some gods have more than one name or look different depending on what they are doing. For example, the sun god can appear three different ways! Unscramble the words in the two columns. See if you can match the time of day to the sun god's appearance.

SIRUNSE   MNA

NNOO   RLEDE

TUSESN   OBY

The Big Cheese

Although there were many hundreds of gods and goddesses, one was a lot more important than all the others. Fill in all the shapes containing the letters G-O-D to see which god was held in the highest esteem!

Hidden Gods

Even if they couldn't be seen, the Egyptians believed that gods were all around them. How many G-O-D words can you find hiding in these sentences?

I don't see any gods...

Long ago, desert winds swept sand through Egypt.

Two woven baskets hung oddly on the good wall.

The golden pagoda had eight gorgeous gongs.

Some cargo delivered yesterday was gone today!

Sad God, Glad God

The gods were responsible for all aspects of life, so it was very important to keep them happy. Make the SAD god into a GLAD god by finding the correct path through the grid. Alternate SAD and GLAD by moving down and up or side to side, but not diagonally. If you hit a MAD god, you are going the wrong way!

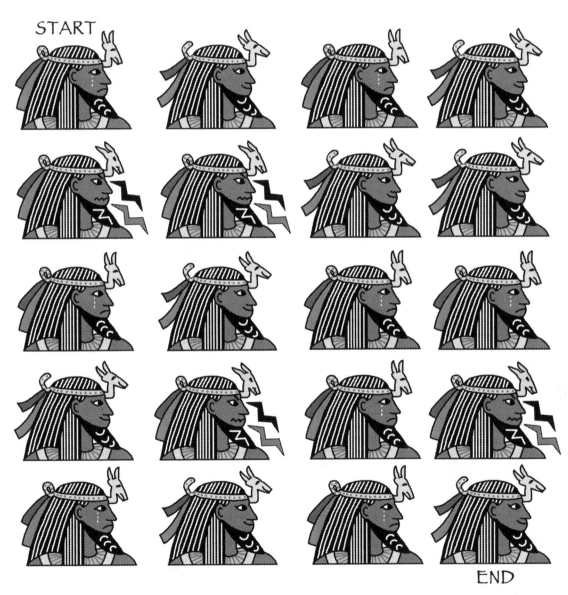

 28

Busy Beetle

Scarab beetles lay their eggs in balls of dung and push them around. To the ancient Egyptians, the scarab beetle represented the god Khepri. Can you guess what they believed was Khepri's responsibility? To find out, write the letters from the scattered pieces into the grid. Hint: Match the pattern of black boxes!

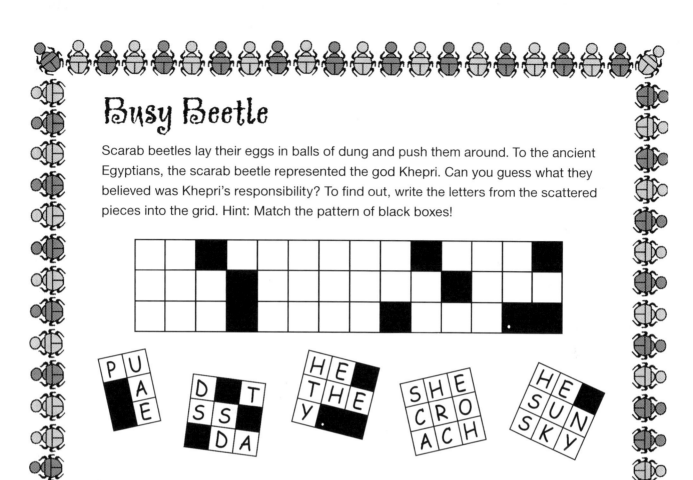

Yuck

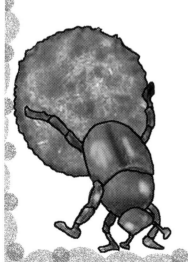

Not exactly sure what "dung" is? Follow the directions and you will soon know!

Scarab beetles push around balls of animal D U N G.

🪲 change the U to O = _ _ _ _

🪲 change the G to P = _ _ _ _

🪲 change the D to P = _ _ _ _

🪲 change the N to O = _ _ _ _

Heads and Tales

Many of the Egyptian gods and goddesses were a combination of a human body with an animal head. Here's your chance to make puppets of some of the most interesting ones!

What you will need:

crayons or markers
scissors
tape
7 pencils or craft sticks

What you do:

☀ Make a copy of the patterns for the gods and goddesses.

☀ Color in the patterns with crayons or markers.

☀ Cut them out on the dotted lines.

☀ Place a puppet face down on the table. Place a craft stick or pencil on the back and attach it with tape to make a handle. Continue until all puppets are made.

☀ Create your own stories to go with the gods and act them out!

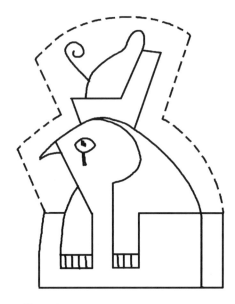

Horus = God of the Sky (falcon). Responsible for the sun and the moon.

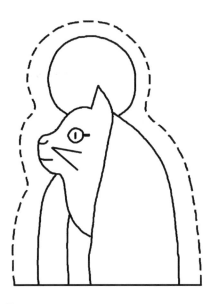

Bast = Goddess of the sunrise (cat). Protector of cats, women and children.

Sobek = God of the Nile (crocodile). Responsible for the fertility the Nile river brought to the land.

Khnum = God of Life (ram). Responsible for the creation of human life.

Anubis = God of the Dead (jackal). Responsible for mummification and guarding the cemeteries.

Thoth = God of Writing (ibis). Responsible for the invention of writing and alphabets.

Sekhmet = War Goddess (lioness). Destroyer of the enemies of Egypt and the pharaohs.

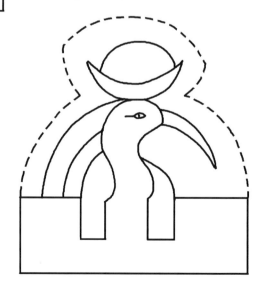

Eye of Horus

Many Egyptians wore charms to protect them from evil or illness. The wedjat eye was one of the most popular. The story is that the eye belonged to the god Horus. It was taken by an evil god who ripped it to pieces. Luckily, the goddess Hathor fixed the eye and returned it to Horus. To see this powerful symbol of healing and protection, copy all the pieces of the wedjat eye into the grid. Hint: Use a thick, dark marker!

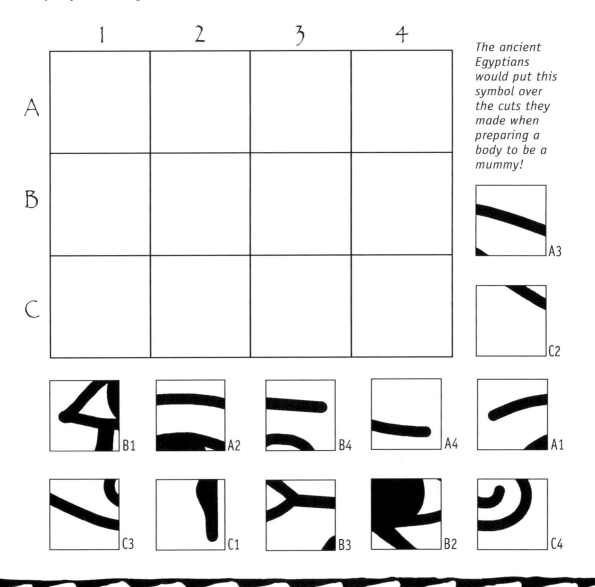

The ancient Egyptians would put this symbol over the cuts they made when preparing a body to be a mummy!

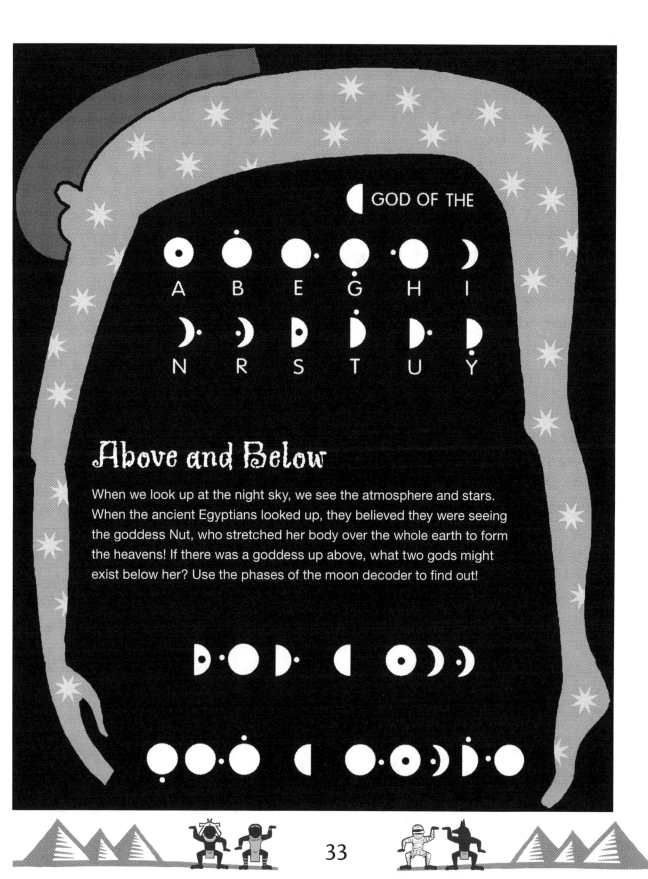

GOD OF THE

A B E G H I

N R S T U Y

Above and Below

When we look up at the night sky, we see the atmosphere and stars. When the ancient Egyptians looked up, they believed they were seeing the goddess Nut, who stretched her body over the whole earth to form the heavens! If there was a goddess up above, what two gods might exist below her? Use the phases of the moon decoder to find out!

Small Protector

Bes was a very short god who had a potbelly, a beard like a lion, and was often shown with his tongue sticking out! His important jobs were to protect women and children and guard the home, especially at night. Many houses had a statue of Bes near the front door. Why? Travel through the maze from START to END. Read the words along the path to learn about this god's surprising way to do his job!

THAT   TO   THAT   HIS   STATUE   WOULD   EYE

HE   AN   MAKE

UGLY   SCARE

HUNGRY

SO   SO   IN

AND

WAS   GODS   EVIL

UGLY   SPIRITS

WAS

HE   AWAY

HE   HE   END   TO

START

1._____

2._____

3._____

4._____

5._____

6._____

Balancing Act

These two goddesses are like two sides of one coin. Bastet is a gentle housecat, and Sekhmet is a fierce lioness! Together they created balance in the ancient world. Take a word and decide which goddess it belongs to. Write it in the column above that goddess. Now find the opposite word and put it over the other goddess. Continue until all the words are sorted and there is balance!

1._____

2._____

3._____

4._____

5._____

6._____

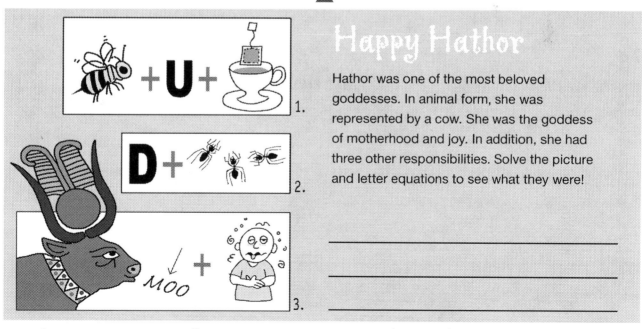

BASTET

FIERCE
DARK
PEACE
NEGATIVE
LIGHT
HEAL
GENTLE
FRIENDS
WAR
ENEMIES
DESTROY
POSITIVE

SEHKMET

Happy Hathor

Hathor was one of the most beloved goddesses. In animal form, she was represented by a cow. She was the goddess of motherhood and joy. In addition, she had three other responsibilities. Solve the picture and letter equations to see what they were!

🐝 +U+ ☕
1.

D+ 🐜🐜🐜
2.

🐄 MOO + 🤢
3.

_____

_____

_____

Before and After

This story was very popular in ancient Egypt:

The story of Osiris gave Egyptians hope for something they really believed in! Each of the clues suggests a word. Write the word on the dotted lines. Then use the fractions to figure out what part of each word to write in the empty boxes. Work from left to right.

Osiris was a good pharaoh who was murdered by his evil brother, Seth. When Seth killed Osiris, he cut the body into pieces and hid them all over Egypt. The wife of Osiris found all the pieces and put Osiris together again. Then, the god Anubis made the repaired body into the first mummy! Osiris went on to become god of the underworld, where he would rule forever.

I just love a story with a happy ending!

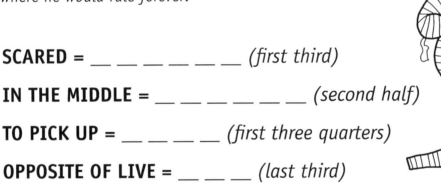

SCARED = __ __ __ __ __ __ *(first third)*

IN THE MIDDLE = __ __ __ __ __ __ *(second half)*

TO PICK UP = __ __ __ __ *(first three quarters)*

OPPOSITE OF LIVE = __ __ __ *(last third)*

The Egyptians made mummies because they believed in an

CHAPTER 4

A BUSY AFTERLIFE

Old Body, New Life

Making a mummy was a long and expensive process. Why did the ancient Egyptians go through all the fuss? To find out, start at the word marked with a dot. Collect every third word clockwise as you circle the mummy.

THAT	DEATH
BODY	FOR
AFTER	A
BELIEVED	– BUT
WHOLE	THIS
AGAIN	PERSON
•THEY	HE
HIS	TO
LIVE	COULD
HAPPEN!	NEEDED

First Class

Pharaohs were the richest and most important people, so they were mummified the best. But their wealth was not the only reason Egyptians took such care with a pharaoh's body! To learn why they got extra special treatment, break the reverse alphabet code (Z=A, Y=B, X= C, etc.) for each word.

K	S	Z	I	Z	L	S	H

Y	V	X	Z	N	V

T	L	W	H

Z	U	G	V	I

W	V	Z	G	S

38

Body Parts

The process of mummification began right after a person's death. Some body parts were removed and stored in special "canopic" jars. Unscramble the letters in each of the four jars. Each one contains the word for an organ that was removed from the pharaoh's body. Once stored in the jar, it was buried alongside the pharaoh.

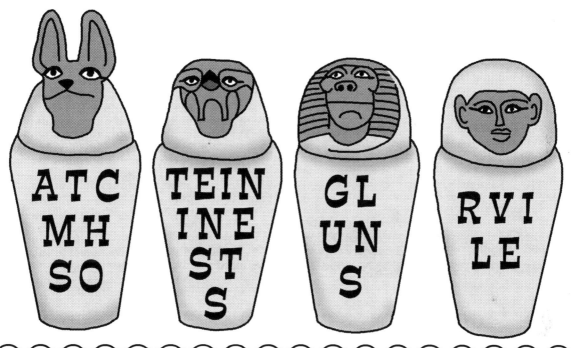

ATC MH SO

TEIN INE STS

GL UN S

RVI LE

This organ was thought to be trash. It was taken out through the nose with a long hook and thrown away!

Ouch!

I love this part!

This organ was believed to be the source of all wisdom. The pharaoh would certainly need this in the afterlife! For that reason, it was never removed from the body.

N B R A I

T A H E R

All Dry

After the organs were removed from a mummy-to-be, it was washed and perfumed. Now the body needed to be dried out—but how? Use a thick marker to cross through all the D-R-Y words in this grid. All three letters must be in a row (side-to-side or up-and-down). Words can overlap. Put the remaining letters on the dotted lines and you will learn what was used to dry out a mummy!

```
D R Y N D R Y A T D R Y D
R R O D R Y N D R Y A K R
Y I D R Y N D R Y D O D Y
D R Y F D R Y D R Y S R A
D R Y D R Y D R Y D R Y L
T D R Y D R Y D R Y D R Y
```

_ _ _ _ _ _ , _ _ _ _ _

_ _ _ _ _ _ .

Say "Aaahh"

Before a mummy was buried, a priest using special tools performed a ceremony. This ceremony made sure that the spirit of the mummy could live, breathe, see, and eat in the afterlife! Solve the picture and letter equations to see what this ritual was called.

O +  + ⌾ **- R**    **- D**   the

Mummy Math

The bandages on this mummy are marked with the letters A, B, C, and D. Write the numbers you find on each bandage on the lines next to their letter. Add the numbers together. Finally, add all the answers together to discover how many days it took the ancient Egyptians to create one mummy.

+8

+29

A

B

D

+10

C

+15

D

+9

-10

C +5

A

+4

B

A. _____ _____ = _____

B. _____ _____ = _____

C. _____ _____ = _____

D. _____ _____ = _____

TOTAL ☐

41

Ba Humbug!

Ancient Egyptians believed that when a person died, his or her unique spirit, or "ba," was set free. This spirit would go looking for the person's life force, or "ka." The ba could only search for the ka at night. During the day it had to return to the mummy of its person! The ba looked like a small bird with the face of the person it belonged to. Match this ba to the correct mummy and get him home as quickly as possible. Hurry up, the sun is rising!

Good Luck

Egyptians wore amulets when they were alive and after their death! They believed these charms would protect them and bring good luck. Many amulets were placed in a mummy's wrappings.

Which amulets are not in both mummies?

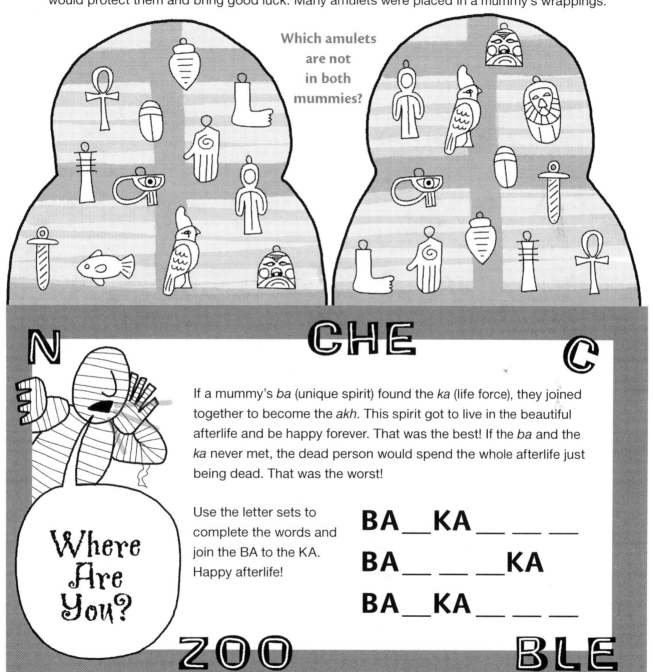

If a mummy's *ba* (unique spirit) found the *ka* (life force), they joined together to become the *akh*. This spirit got to live in the beautiful afterlife and be happy forever. That was the best! If the *ba* and the *ka* never met, the dead person would spend the whole afterlife just being dead. That was the worst!

Use the letter sets to complete the words and join the BA to the KA. Happy afterlife!

BA__KA__ __ __

BA__ __ __KA

BA__KA__ __ __

Where Are You?

Watch Out!

Before it could enjoy the afterlife, the spirit of a dead person faced a terrifying trip through the underworld! This dark place was full of dangers. Break the vowel switch code to learn what some of them were.

HINGRY CRECEDALUS

GAONT SNOKUS

UVAL MENSTURS

FAURY FIRNOCUS

Road Map

Mummies were buried with maps, directions, and magic spells to help them travel safely through the underworld. This info was kept in a special place. To find out where, figure out which letter is missing from each letter set. Write the missing letter in the circle. When you are finished, read the circled letters from top to bottom.

D C A E F ◯
J L K N M ◯
K N L M P ◯
G I H J L ◯

Q S T P R ◯
C A B E D ◯

U S W X V ◯
F I J K G ◯
J G H F I ◯

H F E G C ◯
B A D C F ◯
F E C D B ◯
C B F E G ◯

Careful — some sets have more than one option as an answer!

44

Weigh In

The last test before entering the afterlife took place in the Hall of Judgement. The god Osiris would take something from the dead person and weigh it on a scale against the Feather of Truth. Connect the dots and complete the letters to learn what Osiris would weigh.

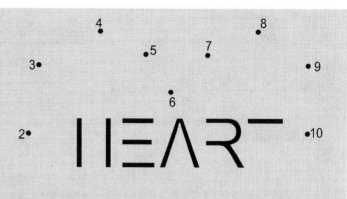

HEART

Phew! I'm glad that part didn't get thrown out!

Gulp!

A monster named Ammut sat by Osiris. It had a crocodile's head, a lion's mane, the front half of a leopard, and the back half of a hippo! If the person being judged had a heart that was heavy with evil, Ammut would make sure he could not enter the afterlife. What would Ammut do? To find out, write the numbered letters into correct boxes of the grid.

1	2	3	4	5	
6	7	8	9	10	

11	12	13	14	15	16	17

	18	19	20		

| | 21 | 22 | 23 | 24 | 25 | ! |

M E O W
2 22 7 17

S H A W L
11 21 23 6 15

W A T E R
12 1 25 20 24

O L D
16 14 10

M U T T
3 8 5 18

H A U L
19 13 4 9

Make It "To Go"

A mummy was buried with many familiar things to provide comfort, both physically and spiritually, in the afterlife. Look for the 16 items hidden in the letter grid.

AMULETS, ANIMALS, BOATS, CLOTHING, FOOD, FURNITURE, GAMES, JEWELRY, MASKS, PERFUME, PETS, POTTERY, SERVANTS, STATUES, TOYS, WEAPONS

```
B O Y R E T T O P W A M U P
S E R V X J E L E W N B X O
B O A T S O S S T Y S O W S
O B A M U L E T S K P A E O
A M U F A Y W S S O O U A E
J E A M X J E A T G T S P M
W G I T L E M R O A T E O U
C N U T U W F U T M O V N F
A I P O M E U S U E X R S R
P H B O A L W A P S U M E E
B T O F U R N I T U R E S P
U O B O K Y N I A M U K Y F
E L T O P D W E A O E S O U
F C Y D T T S E R V A N T S
```

Pretty Pictures

Instead of letters, the ancient Egyptians used a series of pictures and symbols called "hieroglyphs." These pictures spelled out words, showed who or what was being written about, and described actions. When a royal mummy was buried, the walls of the tomb—and even the mummy's coffin—were covered with pictures! These hieroglyphs told all about the person who was buried, especially how successful he was and what a good life he had lived. These stories were one way that the Egyptians tried to win a place in the afterlife!

• • • • • • • • • •

The names of pharaohs were circled with a special rounded rectangle called a "cartouche." Work your way through the maze from START to END. Draw the hieroglyphs you find along the path into the empty cartouche. Use the key to find out which pharaoh is buried here!

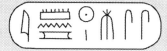 Hatshepsut

 Tutankhamun

 Ramses II

Best Buy

Begin at 72 and count backward by twos. Rearrange and write the letters in this order on the scarabs. When you have finished you will have the silly answer to the joke!

Y	H	T	E
66	70	72	68

C	R	A	S	H	P	U	E
58	60	54	52	56	64	62	50

S	L	O	T
42	48	46	44

F	O
38	40

How do mummies make sure that their money will last forever?

T	R	I	F	F	E	L	A	E
32	28	24	34	22	30	26	36	20

I'm going to put my cash in one of the Nile's river banks!

N	A	N	U	C	I	R	E	S
6	8	16	12	4	18	10	2	14

CHAPTER 5
PUZZLING PYRAMIDS

Hide and Seek

The pharaohs of ancient Egypt were buried in a special tomb called a pyramid. These huge buildings were built from blocks of stone that could weigh up to two tons each! The pharaoh was buried deep inside the pyramid in a special chamber full of gold, jewels, and expensive offerings. It is not surprising that robbers wanted to break in to steal the treasure! For this reason, pyramids had many fake burial chambers and passages that were dead ends. These were supposed to confuse the robbers and keep the treasure—and the pharaoh—hidden.

Can you find your way to the hidden chamber that protects the pharaoh's mummy?

START

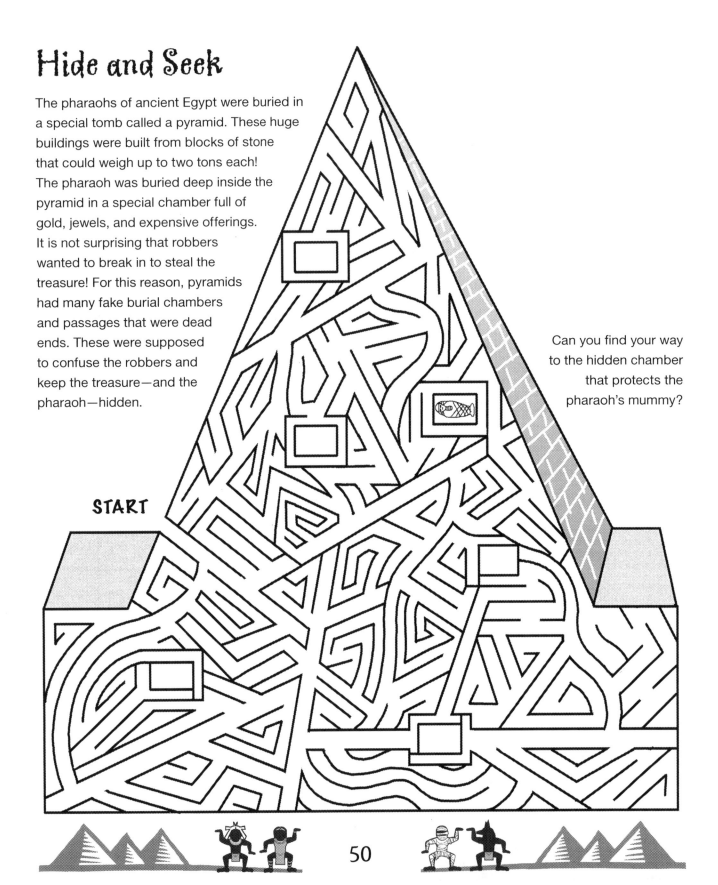

Step It Up

The very first pyramid was built for a pharaoh named Djoser in the year 2650 b.c. That was more than 4,500 years ago! This pyramid did not have the familiar triangular shape of later pyramids. Djoser's monument was constructed with six solid levels, each smaller than the next. That's why his tomb is called the Step Pyramid.

Take the six letters you find around the page. Unscramble them and form a word that means "a strong building material." Write this word in the base of Djoser's pyramid. Remove one letter at a time to form new shorter words all the way to the top where the letter O will sit by itself. On several steps there is more than one word that can be formed.

Use the letters to form a word that means "a strong building material."
Write that word in the bottom step.

Not Just a Builder

The man who designed the step pyramid was born a commoner and became a learned scholar and respected builder. After his death he was worshipped as a god of wisdom and healing! While often remembered as an amazing architect, this man was much more than just a pyramid builder. Use a mirror to learn his name and official titles.

IMHOTEP, Chancellor of the King of Lower Egypt, First after the King of Upper Egypt, Administrator of the Great Palace, Hereditary Nobleman, High Priest of Heliopolis, Builder, Chief Carpenter, Chief Sculptor, and Maker of Vases in Chief.

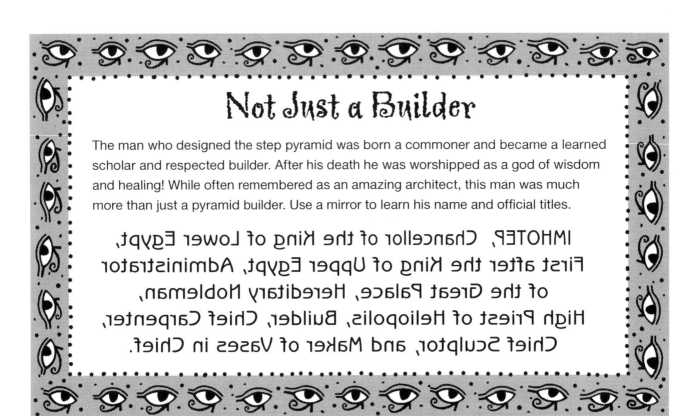

How Odd!

King Snefru was the first pharaoh to build a pyramid with smooth sides. One of his pyramids looked odd because the builders started at a very steep pitch and had to correct the angle halfway through the project. Solve the word fractions to learn the name of this strange pyramid.

Last ⅓ of SCRIBE

Last ⅔ of ANT

First ⅓ of PIE

Last ½ of MY

Middle ½ of CRAB

Last ⅓ of ARM

First ½ of IDEA

Float by Boat

All the stones used in the pyramids had to be brought to the building site from stone quarries. Some limestone could be found nearby, but other stones, like granite, came from far away. Stones were cut at quarries, loaded onto barges, and floated down the Nile to the building site. Steer the barge from the stone quarry to the dock closest to the pyramid.

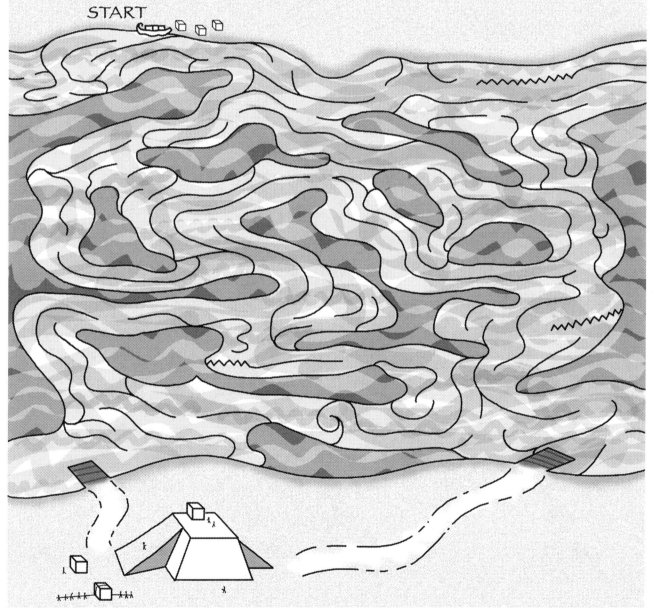

53

All the pyramids were built on the one side of the Nile River, while the cities were built on the other. Why? To find out, take the words scattered on each side of the river and use them to fill in the blanks.

WAS WEST SUN SIDE DEATH WHERE

WHERE LIFE SIDE EAST WAS SUN

THE
_ _ _ _
SIDE,
_ _ _ _ _
THE
_ _ _
SET,
_ _ _ _
THE
_ _ _ _
FOR
_ _ _ _ _ .

THE
_ _ _ _
SIDE,
_ _ _ _ _
THE
_ _ _
ROSE,
_ _ _ _
THE
_ _ _ _
FOR
_ _ _ _ .

We belong on this side!

But the food is better on this side!

Tools of the Trade

A lot of equipment was needed to build a pyramid. Can you find all the tools in the grid?

BONING RODS, CHISEL, CLAMP, HAMMER, MALLET, ROPE, SCAFFOLDING, SLEDS, WEDGE, SAW, POUNDING STONE, LEVEL, PLUMB BOB, SQUARE, LEVER, PICKAX, ROCK DRILL

```
N O R E V E L M B W I S T Y
S A W H P E T U O I S M M P
E F O O R A L M N L Q M X O
L G R O O C D M I M U U Y U
L E V E L L M Y N M A M M N
I Y B T O A C O G W R M M D
R Y O H A M M E R M E Y A I
D M B E T P O X O T L M X N
K M B H E S A M D E A A L G
C U M I D K U D S O F L E S
O M U E C M T I H E I L T T
R E L I M R H P E G D E W O
A S P Y R C M U M M Y T T N
Y Y S C A F F O L D I N G E
```

EXTRA FUN: Find the six times "MUMMY" hidden here too!

55

How High?

The Great Pyramid of Giza, built for a pharaoh named Khufu, is the largest stone structure ever built! It took thousands of workers more than twenty years to construct this massive monument. How tall was it? Cross out all the numbers that contain either a two or a five. Add the remaining numbers together to get the height of the Great Pyramid.

FIVE • 2
75 • SEVEN • 20
HUNDRED • 50
200 • 35 • 7
42 • TWO • 62
100 • 75 • FIVE
HUNDRED • 100
56 • 21 • TWO
SEVEN • 29
20 • FORTY-TWO
50 • FIVE • 60

The Great Pyramid has stood for 4,500 years. In addition to being the largest stone structure ever built, it has another distinction. To find out what it is, crack the last-to-first code and read the words from top to bottom.

TI
SI
HET
NLYO
NEO
FO
HET
EVENS
ONDERSW
FO
HET
NCIENTA
ORLDW
HATT
TILLS
XISTS!E

You know, I always wondered about that!

Paper Pyraminis!

It was hard work to build a real pyramid, but you can have fun creating a miniature version out of paper.

What you need:

card stock (any color)
pencil
ruler
scissors
tape

What you do:

1. Copy the pyramid pattern onto the card stock. You will need one square and four triangles for each pyramid. Cut out the pieces.

2. Line up the base of each triangle with the four sides of the square. Lying flat, the outline will look like a four-pointed star. Tape the pieces in place at the base of each triangle.

3. Lift up two of the triangle sides so that one side of each fits neatly against the other triangle. Tape the two triangles together near the base.

4. Lift the third triangle to meet the other two. Tape it in place near the base. Lift the last triangle to complete the pyramid. Tape it in place near the base.

5. Use a small piece of tape to hold the points at the top together.

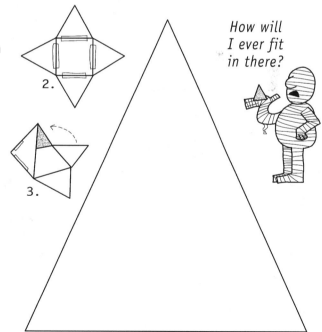

How will I ever fit in there?

People Power

When the pyramids were built, there were no trucks, cranes, or bulldozers. How did all the huge blocks of stone get moved into place? People power, of course! Building the pyramids was hard enough, but around the pyramids were large temples and huge statues. All of this incredibly heavy stuff had to be pulled, pushed, and lifted, too. Phew!

Here is a statue of a pharaoh named Djehutihotep. Add the EVEN numbers inside the monument to learn how many tons it weighs. Add the ODD numbers inside the men to see how many men it took to move it!

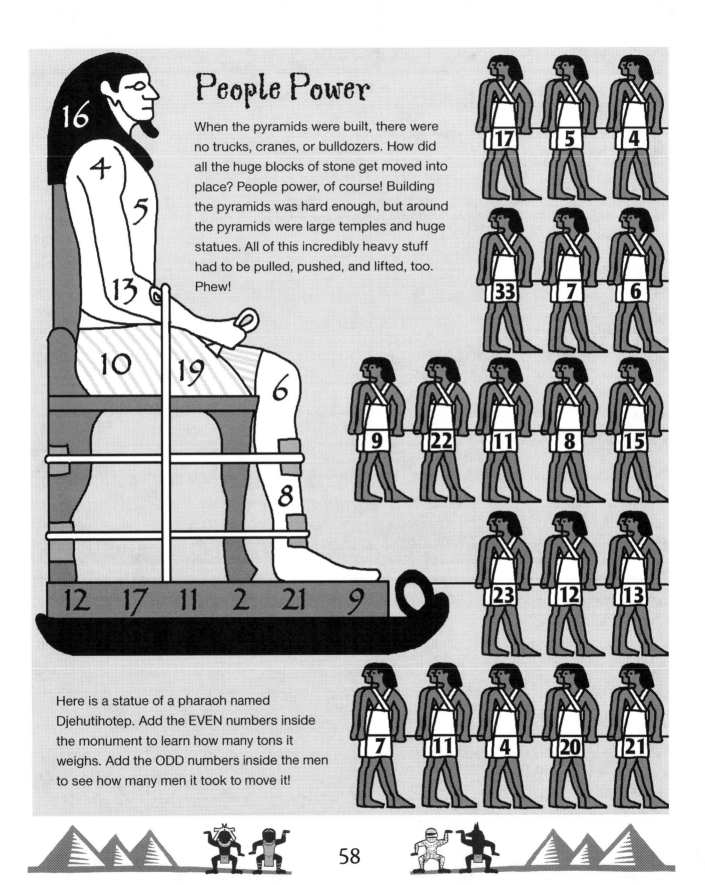

Hidden Ha Ha

Start at the square with the dot. Follow the arrows to spell a pyramid joke and its silly answer. If you land on a square with no arrow, keep going in the same direction until the next arrow.

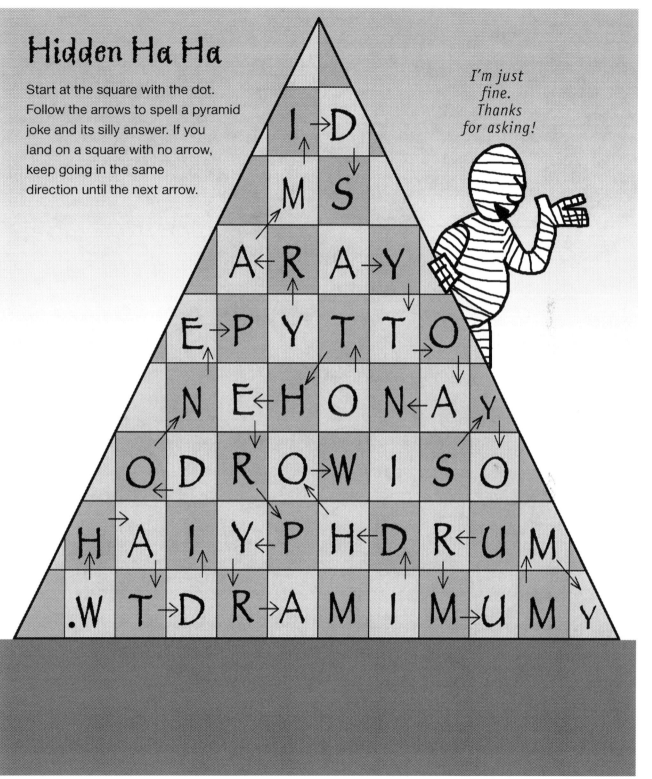

I'm just fine. Thanks for asking!

No More Pyramids?

The age of building pyramids ended about 2150 B.C. After that, many pharaohs were buried in the Valley of the Kings. A large and important burial ground such as this had a special name. To learn what it is, complete this puzzle. Each clue suggests a word. Write each word into its proper space on the tombs. When you have finished, read the shaded tombs in order. Hint: The last letter of one answer is the first letter for the next one!

1. Number after eight
2. Foreign and unusual
3. Seat at a desk

4. Cowboy skills show
5. Partly on top of
6. Musical instrument with keys

7. Wise night-bird
8. Necklace of flowers from Hawaii
9. Twelve of these make a foot

Think there's room for us?

Break the vowel switch code to discover another name for this giant cemetery!

"CATY EF THU DUOD"

60

CHAPTER 6
TREASURES OF THE TOMBS

Finding Tut's Tomb

For seven years, Howard Carter searched for King Tut's tomb. His boss finally told him to quit looking, but Carter talked him into letting him search for one more season. In 1922, on his last dig, Howard Carter found it! Even though it seemed that tomb robbers had broken in twice, an amazing amount of treasure was still in the tomb. Start digging through LAYERS OF SAND, work your way through the RUBBLE, and find Carter's path through the rest of the maze to the word TREASURY.

LAYERS OF SAND

ANCIENT

WORKER'S

HUTS

BURIED STAIRS

BURIAL CHAMBER

THE SENTINELS

TREASURY

CORRIDOR FILLED WITH RUBBLE

62

I Spy Treasure

Find the three groups of treasure in the grid.

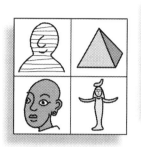
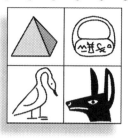

63

R Is for Royalty

Royal families were prepared for the afterlife by filling their tombs with many possessions—full-sized items, miniature items, and items represented in paintings. Search this tomb for things that start with the letter R. Which of them would a pharaoh recognize? Which things are too modern or don't belong in Egypt?

Pet Packages

Egyptians embalmed animals just as they did people! Some of these animals were sacrifices to the gods, but others were beloved pets meant to go with their owners into the afterlife. Unscramble the names of some common animals that were mummified. Match each name to the correct mummy.

___ OGD

___ ATC

___ NOABBO

___ DICROOLEC

___ TBARBI

___ NOAFLC

___ SIBI

A

B

C

D

E

F

G

Choosing a Coffin

Before being buried, the mummy was put in a stone coffin called a sarcophagus. Each sarcophagus was decorated to resemble what the mummy looked like when he or she was a living person! Can you find the sarcophagus that has all of these characteristics?

- **striped headdress**
- **false beard**
- **eyes look up**
- **hieroglyphs**

Hieroglyph Sudoku

Hieroglyphs were the Egyptian form of picture writing. They were often painted on the coffin, or sarcophagus, of a mummy. These hieroglyphs would tell marvelous stories about the life—and afterlife—of the person buried in a tomb.

Hieroglyphs could be read either vertically or horizontally. Fill in the boxes using the different hieroglyphs. Each picture must appear only ONCE in each row going across, ONCE in each column going up and down, and ONCE in each group of four boxes created by the darker lines.

Here are the four hieroglyphs to choose from.

67

Precious Past

Modern Egyptian archaeologists work very hard to conserve and restore the precious treasures from ancient times. The head of Egypt's Supreme Council of Antiquities has spent his career committed to preserving discoveries, old and new, so that history will not be lost. Who is this notable man? Each of the clues below suggests a word. Write the answers onto the dotted lines and read the first letter of each word from top to bottom. They will spell out his name.

Black and white
   striped animal = __ __ __ __ __

Fruit for cider = __ __ __ __ __

Japanese poetry = __ __ __ __ __

House of snow = __ __ __ __ __

Opposite of sad = __ __ __ __ __

Nut of the oak tree = __ __ __ __ __

Liquid that falls as rain = __ __ __ __ __

Opposite of below = __ __ __ __ __

To frighten = __ __ __ __ __

Not easy to bend = __ __ __ __ __

68

Hidden Chamber

The burial chamber of a pharaoh was filled with precious objects. Inside the pyramid or tomb, the real burial chamber was often hidden among many other chambers to confuse robbers! Use the clues to figure out which chamber holds the body of the pharaoh.

The pharaoh is buried in a chamber with a crown.
There are no more than two crowns in its row or its column.
The chamber has a heart to the left and to the right.

👑	❤️	⭐	👑	❤️
⭐	👑	❤️	❤️	⭐
❤️	👑	👑	❤️	👑
👑	❤️	👑	⭐	⭐
⭐	👑	❤️	⭐	👑
👑	⭐	❤️	👑	❤️

69

Mummy Madness

You can understand why tomb robbers would steal gold jewelry. But why steal a mummy? Well, for hundreds of years, mummies were used all over Europe. In fact, they were so popular that the supply of real mummies ran short. Creative peddlers would make "new" mummies using any dead body they could find! To learn why people were so interested in stealing, buying, and using mummies, read the clues below. Each one suggests a word. Write that word on the dotted lines and transfer the letters into the numbered grid.

1G	2A R	3I	4B	5H	6C		7B	8H	9B	10J	11F		12H	13D	14J	
15A U	16F	17D	18A D		19E	20I		21J	22J	23K	24L	25C				
26H	27B	28L	29I	30K			31G	32D	33K	34C	35L			36L	37E	38D
39J	40A E	41F	42K	43G	44I ,	45H		46B	47J	48A N	49C	50C ,	51L	!		

A. Opposite of over

$\underline{U}_{15}$ $\underline{N}_{48}$ $\underline{D}_{18}$ $\underline{E}_{40}$ $\underline{R}_{2}$

B. Kids' stomach

$\overline{46}$ $\overline{4}$ $\overline{7}$ $\overline{9}$ $\overline{27}$

C. Young person

$\overline{50}$ $\overline{25}$ $\overline{49}$ $\overline{34}$ $\overline{6}$

D. A brainstorm

$\overline{32}$ $\overline{38}$ $\overline{17}$ $\overline{13}$

E. Opposite of out

$\overline{19}$ $\overline{37}$

F. To speak

$\overline{16}$ $\overline{41}$ $\overline{11}$

G. Animal that oinks

$\overline{31}$ $\overline{43}$ $\overline{1}$

H. Past tense of swing

$\overline{26}$ $\overline{12}$ $\overline{8}$ $\overline{5}$ $\overline{45}$

I. Person, place, or thing

$\overline{44}$ $\overline{3}$ $\overline{29}$ $\overline{20}$

J. Kiss

$\overline{14}$ $\overline{10}$ $\overline{22}$ $\overline{47}$ $\overline{21}$ $\overline{39}$

K. Opposite of push

$\overline{30}$ $\overline{23}$ $\overline{33}$ $\overline{42}$

L. Green lawn plant

$\overline{24}$ $\overline{28}$ $\overline{36}$ $\overline{35}$ $\overline{51}$

70

Just Joking

A riddle and its silly answer were put into a grid, then cut into pieces. See if you can figure out where each piece goes, and write the letters in their proper places. Hint: Use the pattern of the black boxes.

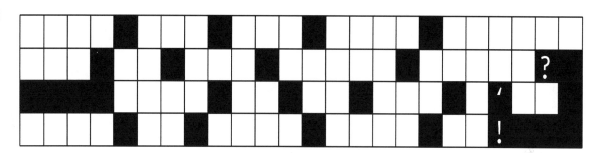

Aren't you forgetting something??

What did you stuff this guy with? Rocks?

Small yet Special

Many small items were placed in the tombs with the pharaohs. Some were amulets to guard them. Others were riches to provide for them in the afterlife. There were jewelry, weapons, small statues, and even toys!

- ☀ How many different treasures are shown here?
- ☀ Which item is pictured the most?
- ☀ Which is pictured only once?

CHAPTER 7

MUMMY FEVER

Hinky Pinkies

The answers to hinky pinkies are two rhyming words that each have two syllables.

What do you call a mummy who...

...is made out of sticky candy?

_ _ _ _ _ _   _ _ _ _ _

...is very friendly?

_ _ _ _ _ _ _   _ _ _ _ _

...eats crackers in bed?

_ _ _ _ _ _ _   _ _ _ _ _ _

...is not very smart?

_ _ _ _ _ _ _   _ _ _ _ _ _

What do you call ...

...a mummy's favorite card game?

_ _ _ _ _ _ _   _ _ _ _ _

...where a mummy's navel is?

_ _ _ _ _ _ _   _ _ _ _ _

74

Dead and Gone

There are many words that mean the same thing as "dead." Four of them are hidden in this letter grid. To find them, take one letter from each column moving from left to right. Each letter can only be used once, so cross them off as you use them.

What does "dead" mean?

How would I know?

P	E	F	E	A	E	E	S
D	E	R	A	S	T	E	D
L	E	C	I	L	S	E	D
D	I	P	E	R	H	S	D

1. _____

2. _____

3. _____

4. _____

Signed Copies

All of these children's authors have written books with mummy themes. Four of them have signed these books. Part of an author's first name is on the top line and part of his last name is on the bottom line. Can you figure out which author signed which book?

1. Ron Roy
2. James Preller
3. Mary Pope Osborne
4. Kate McMullan
5. Philip Yates
6. R. L. Stine
7. Wendelin Van Draanen

Trick or Treat

Mummy costumes are fun at Halloween! This kid has been wrapped tight in T.P. Can you find your way from START to END?

START

You're Covered

Kara has a dozen rolls of toilet paper. Each of the rolls contains 115 feet of paper. If Kara needs 5,520 inches of toilet paper to wrap each person, how many of her friends can she turn into mummies for Halloween?

Wow! That's a major mummy!

END

Fright Night

What scary movie are these kids watching? Fill in all the shapes that contain the letters P-O-P-C-O-R-N to find out!

EEK!

I don't think this is scary, do you?

Tons o' Mummies

Sometimes, the priests of ancient Egypt would gather a bunch of different mummies and move them all to a single, hidden tomb. They did this to try to outsmart the tomb robbers! It could get confusing with all the mummies jumbled together. Can you tell how many mummies are hidden here?

Show Offs

You don't have to travel to Egypt to see mummies. Many museums around the world have Egyptian exhibits! Can you find the eight countries hidden in the grid?

```
T H E E M A M
I S N R I E T Y N
H N T E E A R R C O U
E S W I T Z E R L A N D H
U A E W O H R S L D T H A T A
M U N I T E D S T A T E S E V
N S G T H R B I T S O F E G Y
A T L T A L I I G R E E C E P
I R A D T A H M M Y M N A I T
T I N L Y N A M R E G F E X H
P A D R E D X G E O S T I B I
H A O V S C O T L A N D G
T H M E R I E A R E Y
W A Y E R T S I N
N C O U N T H
```

**AUSTRIA
ENGLAND
GERMANY
GREECE
NETHERLANDS
SCOTLAND
SWITZERLAND
UNITED STATES**

The crumbling mummy of the pharaoh Ramses II was flown to Paris for a bit of fixing up. On the trip, he used something that no other royal mummy had ever used before. What was it? Break the vowel switch code to find out!

HAS EWN POSSPERT

79

Love My Tunes

To find the answer to this riddle, cross out any letters that appear three or more times. Collect the leftover letters from left to right and top to bottom and write them in the blanks.

What does a mummy listen to on his radio?

B	G	K	O	V	D	X	V	J	Q	E	H
H	L	W	J	T	B	F	L	K	R	B	N
F	Q			G	A	N					F
N	X		Z	H	O						G
P	K		V	X	E						D
Z	T		D	Z	M						U
O	E	H	S	T	X	L	T	J	I	O	Q
V	B	Q	J	E	N	C	G	L	D	F	K

___ ___ ___ ___ ___   ___ ___ ___ ___

Take a Dip

To find the silly answer to the riddle, name the pictures at the top of the puzzle. Follow the line from each picture to a box at the bottom. Write the first letter of the picture in the box!

Where do mummies like to go swimming?

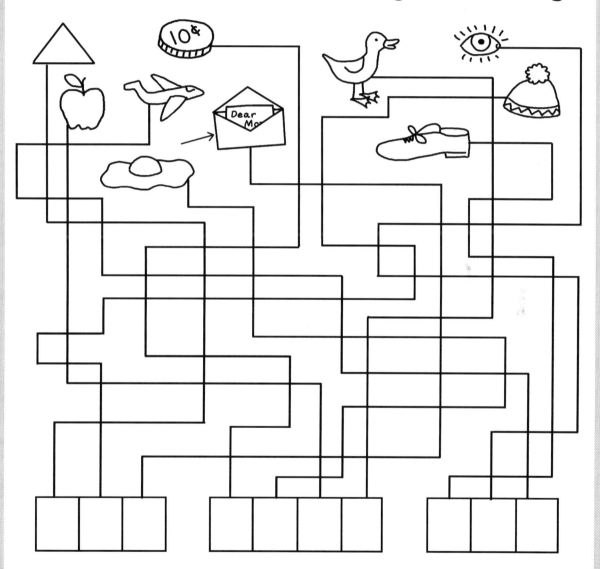

Fun Field Trip

These kids are fascinated by the Egyptian exhibit. There is so much to look at! The small pictures on the following page are part of this bigger picture below. Look closely and decide where each small piece came from. Find the letter and number that correspond to that box and write them in the blanks under each small picture. We've done the first one for you!

 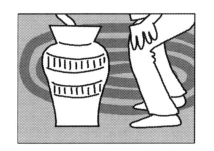 

C 2   __ __   __ __

__ __   __ __   __ __

__ __   __ __   __ __

 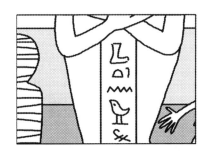 

__ __ __   __ __   __ __

83

What U Need 2 B

1. Fill in all of the blocks on the left side of each sign.
2. Fill in all the blocks across the top of signs 2 and 3.
3. Fill in all the blocks across the bottom of sign 2.
4. Fill in all the blocks on the right side of sign 3.
5. Fill in the center block of signs 2 and 3.
6. Fill in the middle three blocks on the right side of signs 1 and 4.

What is the most important thing you need to be a mummy?

CHAPTER 8

Ancient Egypt, Then and Now

A Modern Mummy

This activity will give you an idea of the work it took to make a mummy!

You will need:

- 1 dead pharaoh
  (a small banana, not too ripe)
- a sacred adze (sharp kitchen knife)
- brain hook (tiny spoon)
- natron (1 box table salt and
  2 small boxes of baking soda)

- linen (first-aid gauze)
- amulet (small paperclip)
- stuffing (scraps of cloth)
- sarcophagus (narrow, banana-length
  tray made from tin foil)
- mask (white sticky label, magic marker)

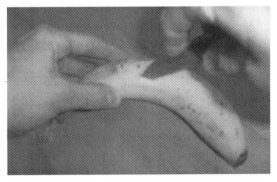

1. Have an adult help you cut a flap in the side of the "pharaoh."

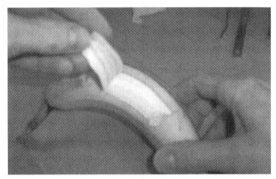

2. Gently peel back the flap.

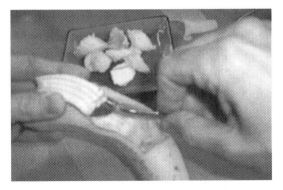

3. Use the tiny spoon to scoop out all the banana. Be gentle but thorough!

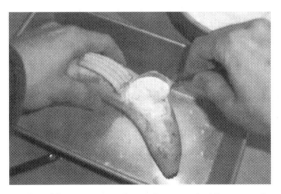

4. Combine 1 cup salt and 1 cup baking powder. Pack as much as you can into the pharaoh.

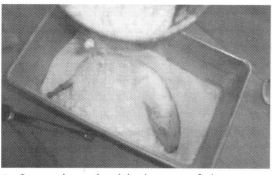

5. Cover pharaoh with the rest of the natron. Mix more if you need to. Put the pharaoh in a dry place for 30 days.

6. Scoop all the natron out of the dry pharaoh. Stuff with scraps of fabric.

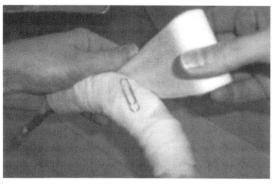

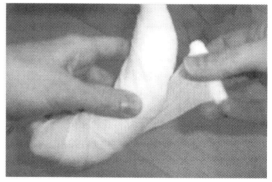

7. Wrap the pharaoh in linen. Place the amulet over the flap and wrap in place.

8. Continue to wrap the pharaoh neatly with several layers. Tuck the end in place.

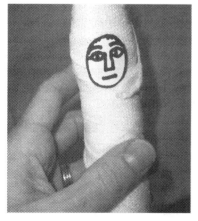

9. Make a mask of the pharaoh with a sticky label and marker.

10. Make a sarcophagus out of a double layer of foil. Use fabric scraps to tuck the pharaoh in.

Picture Play

Ancient Egyptians liked to play picture and counting games. They would have loved the sudoku puzzles that are so popular today! Follow these rules to fill in the boxes using the four different hieroglyphs.

Each picture can only appear...
...once in each row going across
...once in each column going up and down
...once in each group of four boxes created
    by the darker lines

Here are the four hieroglyphs to choose from.

Great Games

Kids in ancient Egypt played a game where they would jump over the arms of two playmates whose hands were touching. The game got more difficult each time the playmates raised their arms! Crack the number substitution code (1=A, 2=B, 3=C, etc.) to find out the name of the Egyptian game and the name of a similar game that kids in this country still play today.

Kids in ancient Egypt played a game called

11~8~21~26~26~1

12~1~23~9~26~26~1

Kids today play a game called

12-5-1-16-6-18-15-7

Pyramid Power

There is an Egyptian pyramid hiding in your house. It's green and can be folded. You can trade this ancient symbol for modern products such as candy, soda, or a newspaper. Where is it? Use the hieroglyph decoder to find the answer!

A ◎

B ⌐

E ⚚

I 👁

N △

L 🦋

O 🧍

🧍△ T H⚚ L◎CK

🧍F ◎ 🧍△⚚

D🧍🦋🦋◎R L👁🦋🦋

Popular Pyramids

Around the world, pyramids are still being built! These buildings are used as hotels and office buildings, not burial places. Perhaps the most famous modern pyramid is the new entrance to the Louvre Museum in Paris, built in 1989.

Unlike the pyramids of ancient Egypt, the pyramid at the Louvre was not made from blocks of stone. To learn which modern materials were used, make a three-letter word in each column by placing a letter in the empty middle box. Choose from the letters underneath each grid. The words you make will read from top to bottom. When you are done, read across the shaded rows from left to right for the answer.

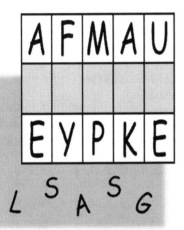

A	F	M	A	U
E	Y	P	K	E

L S A S G

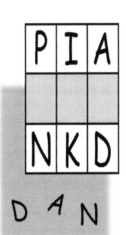

P	I	A
N	K	D

D A N

A	A	R	B	A
H	E	D	T	L

T S L E E

Connect the dots to find out how another modern pyramid in Las Vegas is used.

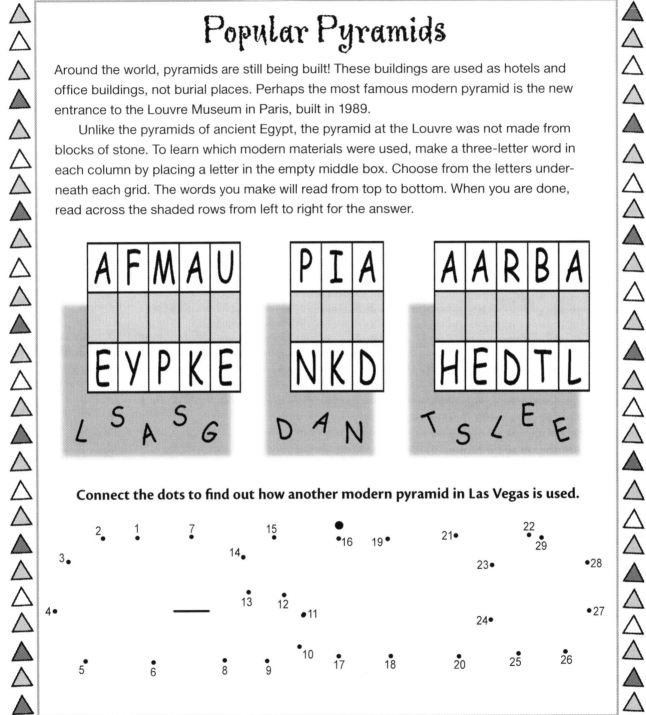

90

It's a Plan

An artist has designed a very creative paper pyramid. Which one of these flat patterns will fold up into the finished pyramid?

What will they think of next?

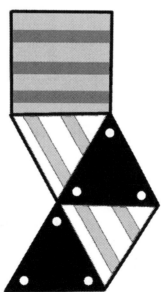

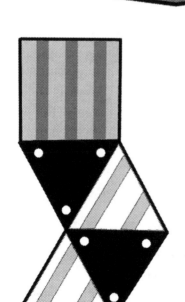

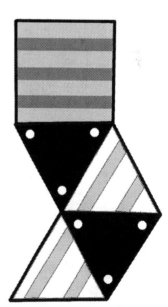

Medicine Man

The earliest record of a physician was found in ancient Egypt. The name of this first doctor was Hesyre, and he practiced medicine during the time of pharaoh Djoser, more than 4,000 years ago! Hesyre was respected and had a very impressive title. Can you break the flip-flop code to learn what it was?

CHIEF OF DENTISTS AND PHYSICIANS

Dr., Dr.

Color in all the letters that are NOT vowels. Write them on the lines in the order that you find them in the grid, from left to right and top to bottom. This strange bunch of letters spells out the ancient Egyptian word for "doctor"! Look in the answer key to see how it is pronounced.

A E I S O U A
O U I E U O W
I N E A U I A U
E I A E W O U

___ ___ ___ ___ ___

"One-quarter of what you eat keeps you alive. The other three-quarters keeps your doctor alive." *This saying was found in an ancient Egyptian tomb. It could easily be said about modern people and the bad eating habits that make them unhealthy!*

Wow!

The fertile ground along the Nile River was perfect for growing things, but the heavy clay soil made planting seeds difficult. More than 5,000 years ago, the Egyptians invented something to make planting much easier, and farmers all over the world still use it today! Transfer the pattern from each box into the grid to learn the name of this handy tool and the strong helper needed to move it.

That was easy!

	A	B	C	D
1				
2				
3				
4				

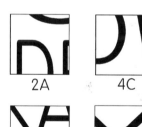

2A   4C

3B   1C

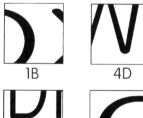

3C   3D   2C   1D   1B   4D

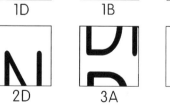

4A   2B   4B   2D   3A   1A

   93

HIEROGLYPHS

Say What?

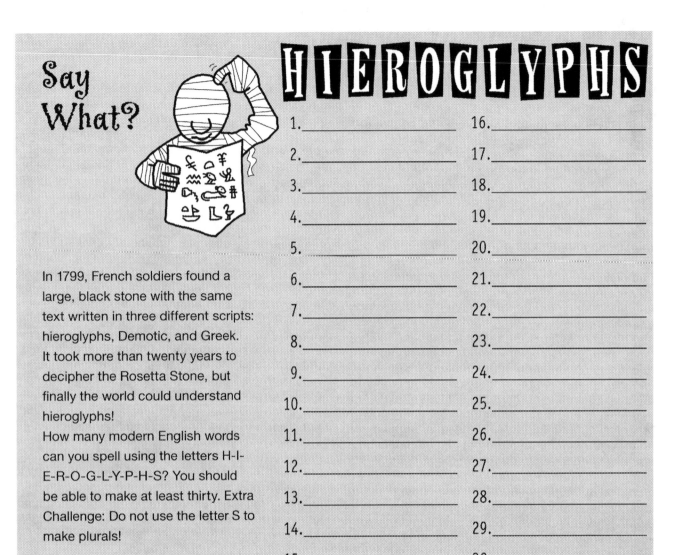

In 1799, French soldiers found a large, black stone with the same text written in three different scripts: hieroglyphs, Demotic, and Greek. It took more than twenty years to decipher the Rosetta Stone, but finally the world could understand hieroglyphs!

How many modern English words can you spell using the letters H-I-E-R-O-G-L-Y-P-H-S? You should be able to make at least thirty. Extra Challenge: Do not use the letter S to make plurals!

1._____   16._____
2._____   17._____
3._____   18._____
4._____   19._____
5._____   20._____
6._____   21._____
7._____   22._____
8._____   23._____
9._____   24._____
10._____   25._____
11._____   26._____
12._____   27._____
13._____   28._____
14._____   29._____
15._____   30._____

Money Before Money

People of ancient Egypt did not use coins or bills like we do. Grain was the most important way to pay for things. State "granaries" (where grain was stored) functioned as banks!

Study the picture on the facing page. Count the bundles of grain each person carries. Now look at the price tags on the items in the market and figure out what each person can buy with his or her grain. Here's the hard part: try to complete the puzzle so that all the grain from each person is spent and everything in the market has been bought! There can be more than one answer.

A. _____ B. _____ C. _____ D. _____ E. _____

_____ _____ _____ _____ _____

_____ _____ _____ _____ _____

_____ _____ _____ _____ _____

Cool Clothing

The Egyptians were the first to wear cloth woven from the fibers of the flax plant. We still wear this kind of fabric today! Egyptian men wore fitted tunics (long, straight shirts) that fell to their knees. Women's tunics looked the same except they reached their ankles. The fabric was almost always white. This kept the Egyptians cool and was less expensive and easier to make than colored fabric!

To learn the name of this fabric, look at the small picture above each Egyptian. Circle the first letter of the picture on each tunic. Read the circled letters from left to right.

CHAPTER 9

High Tech
Meets the Mummy

Safely Scientific

Many high-tech tools have been invented to help scientists safely study the living human body. Machines have also been developed to help organize and study the huge amount of information these tools provide. When modern scientists wanted to study fragile mummies without harming them, they tried using the same tools. It worked great! Now they could see inside all kinds of ancient and very delicate artifacts without having to cut them apart. Can you carefully place the tools into their proper places in the crisscross grid?

COMPUTER, CT SCAN, DNA TEST, ENDOSCOPE, MICROSCOPE, ROBOT, X-RAY, XEROGRAPH, CAMERA

It won't hurt!

No way!!

Royal X-ray

How can an x-ray let us know if a mummy was royal or not? Collect all the letters that are not Xs from left to right and top to bottom. Write them in the spaces provided.

FUN FACT: Scientists have x-rayed the skulls of royal mummies to help figure out which mummies are related to each other!

Do we know him?

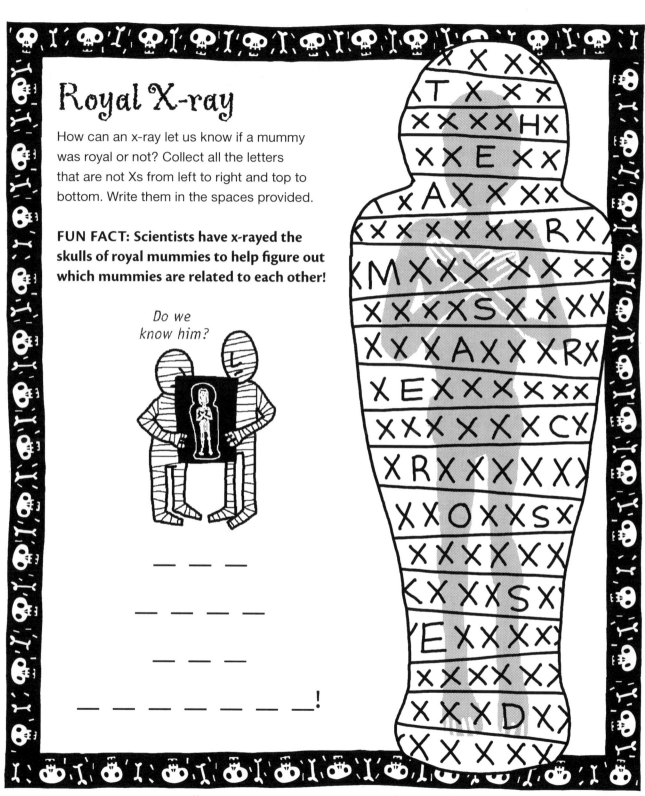

_ _ _

_ _ _ _

_ _ _

_ _ _ _ _ _ _!

Taking a Peek

An endoscope is a tiny camera on a slender tube that is used to see inside a body without cutting it. It is particularly helpful in studying mummies because it doesn't damage them. While exploring inside the lungs of Egyptian mummies, scientists found something very interesting!

Find the letter sets that are hiding in the border of this page. Use them to complete all of the END words. Then read the circled letters from top to bottom to see what the mummies' lungs contained.

To go on forever = E N D _ _ _ _

Light purple = _ _ _ _ E N D _ _

Warm and pleasant = _ _ _ _ E N D _ _

Machine to mix food = _ _ _ E N D _ _

Positive ID

In 2003, scientists used a powerful scientific tool to identify a no-name mummy in Atlanta, Georgia. He turned out to be Pharaoh Ramses I! After the discovery, Ramses was returned to his home in Egypt. To learn which process gave Ramses back his name, decide if each statement is TRUE or FALSE. Circle the letter under the correct column, then take the letters from top to bottom and write them on the dotted lines.

	TRUE	FALSE
The weather in Egypt is cold.	R	D
Pharoahs were kings.	N	O
Egyptians worshipped many gods.	A	P
Amulets were worn for bad luck.	S	T
A pyramid could be built in a year.	U	E
King Tut's tomb held many treasures.	S	C
A sarcophagus is a stone coffin.	T	N
Making a mummy took 3 days.	E	I
There is a pyramid on a US dollar.	N	L
It was an easy journey to the Afterlife.	D	G

— — — — — — — — — — — —

Hey cousin! How ya doing?

WELCOME HOME RAMSES!

101

What a Nose!

Even in death, the mummy of Ramses II had a dignified profile.
How did the ancient Egyptians who made the mummy keep
Ramses' nose from getting all squished? A xeroradiograph (a picture
of the body like an x-ray but on paper instead of film) revealed their
secret. Crack the keyboard code to find out what it was!

Y8W HQWQO DQF856

2QW W57RR3E 285Y

*3**34D94HW!

Write Like an Egyptian

There are several websites where you can enter text and have it translated into the ancient Egyptians' picture writing (see Appendix B). That is a very high-tech way to create hieroglyphs! This activity is a bit more low-tech. We've given you a chart of hieroglyphs. Use colored markers or pencils to write your name at the bottom of the page!

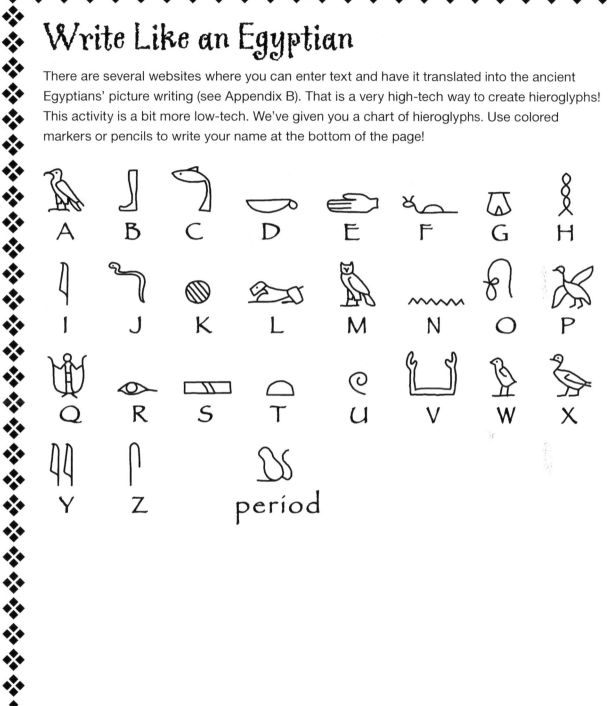

Modern Mummies?

Two technologies currently exist that might have fascinated the ancient Egyptians. Both are used to preserve bodies after death. Solve the word fractions to see how these processes work.

In the process called **PLASTINATION**, water and fat in the body are replaced by...

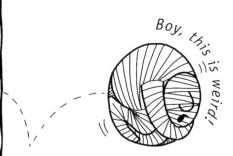

Boy, this is weird!

First 3/4 of PLAY = __ __ __

Last 1/2 of MOST = __ __

Second 1/4 of FIND = __

First 1/3 of COW = __

In the process called **CRYONICS**, the body is preserved by...

BRRRR! This is awful!!

First 2/3 of FRY = __ __

Middle 1/2 of NEED = __ __

First 1/4 of ZERO = __

Middle 1/2 of MIND = __ __

Last 1/5 of CLANG = __

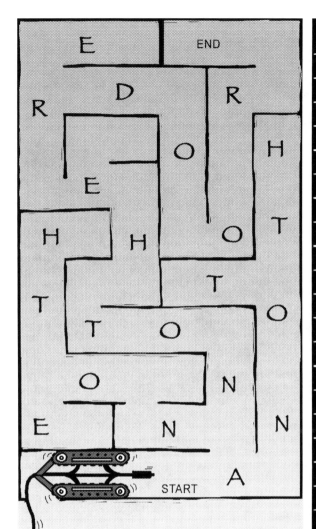

Go, Rover!

Small robots can crawl through tiny places and take pictures where people cannot fit. One rover crawled more than 200 feet up a narrow shaft inside the Pyramid of Khufu. Its goal was to drill through a stone door. What was on the other side? Read the letters in order as you help the rover climb!

Cause of Death

There are scientists who love studying mummies to learn about the diseases ancient Egyptians lived with—and died from! There is a name for this kind of specialist. To find out what it is, put the words in alphabetical order, then read the shaded boxes from top to bottom.

JOLLY

DEAD

BRAG

DOWN

PASS

NICE

RATE

FLAME

COLD

HORN

DRIP

GHOST

LOST

APPLE

MAGIC

GATE

Close Encounters

Which mummy parts are getting a very close look from the x-ray machine?

1.

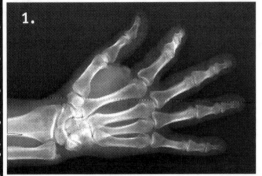

2.

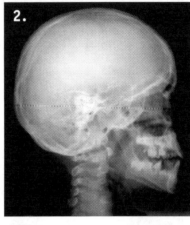

3.

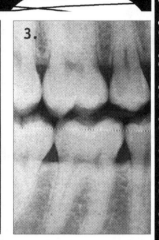

4.

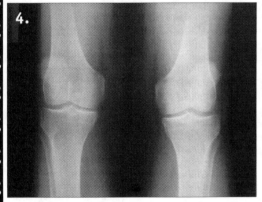

5.

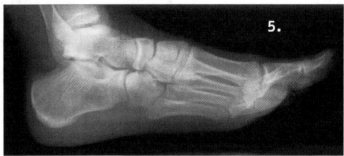

6.

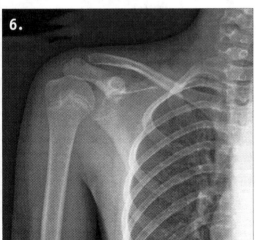

7.

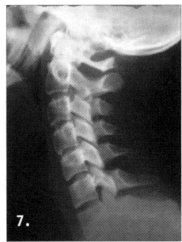

8.

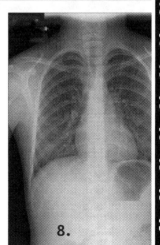

Closed for Repair

Each year one of the pyramids at Giza is closed for restoration work. This is necessary because salt builds up on the inside walls, sometimes as thick as three-quarters of an inch! What causes this buildup? Cross off some of the words according to the directions. When you have finished, read the words that remain from left to right and top to bottom.

Egyptian monuments have always needed repairs. Pharaoh Khufu wrote how he had the headdress of the Great Sphinx fixed after it had been hit by lightning!

Cross out:
— 5 colors
— 4 animals
— 4 flowers
— 3 foods

BLUE

THE DAISY

CAT MILK COW

BREATH PURPLE RED

OF MONKEY TULIP SO

GREEN YELLOW MANY BEANS

LILY DOG VISITORS BANANA IRIS

Dead End

Which of the shadows exactly matches our ancient friends?

Look Again!

You finished the last puzzle in the last chapter—did you think the book was over?
Surprise! Here in the afterlife (known as the appendix) you have one more puzzle to do!
Find each picture piece somewhere in this book. Write the name of the puzzle each
piece is from next to the number. Hint: There is only one piece from each chapter.

1.

2.

3.

4.

Think there's room for us?

5.

6.

7.

8.

9.

GLOSSARY AND RESOURCE LIST

GLOSSARY

afterlife
The place ancient Egyptians believed you went to after death.

amulet
A lucky charm.

archaeologist
A person who studies the remains of past human life.

CT scan
A 3-D image made by x-ray cameras and computers.

dig
A search by archaeologists for ancient artifacts they believe are buried under the ground.

hieroglyphs
The picture writing of ancient Egyptians.

mummification
A process to preserve a dead body from decay.

pharaoh
An ancient Egyptian king or queen.

pyramid
A burial monument with a square base and four sides that rise to a point.

sarcophagus
An outer coffin made of stone.

BOOKS

Jill Rubalcaba, *Ancient Egypt: Archaelogy Unlocks the Secrets of Egypt's Past* (2007)
A National Geographic publication that focuses on how archaeologists have tried to learn as much as possible about ancient Egypt and the people who lived at that time.

Roberta Edwards, *Who Was King Tut?* (2006)
An illustrated biography about the famous boy king of ancient Egypt.

Nicholas Reeves, *Into the Mummy's Tomb* (1992)
This is a true account of Howard Carter's discovery of the tomb of King Tutankhamun. It describes in detail the treasures within and includes many photographs of this spectacular find.

Sandra Markle, *Outside and Inside Mummies* (2005)
This stunning book shows the newest ways scientists can study and learn from mummies.

110

FILMS

The Mummy
Universal Pictures (1932)
This classic horror movie stars Boris Karloff as the Egyptian prince Imhotep, who was buried alive. The movie is set in the 1920s, when a group of archaeologists accidentally awakens Imhotep.

The Mummy (1999)
Universal Pictures
A 1999 remake of the original film stars Brendan Fraser, Rachel Weisz, and lots of special effects.

The Mummy Returns (2001)
Universal Pictures
The sequel to the popular 1999 movie sees Fraser and Weisz battle Imhotep and the Scorpion King.

The Mummy: Tomb of the Dragon Emperor (2008)
Universal Pictures
In this third installment of the *Mummy* franchise, the action shifts to China, where the archaeologists awaken an ancient emperor.

WEBSITES

National Geographic
www.nationalgeographic.com
A search of "Ancient Egypt" on this interactive site will give you many links to pages with stunning video and photographs of pyramids, mummies, tomb treasures, and other artifacts. Look for the translator. It changes the words you type on the virtual keyboard into hieroglyph certificates and postcards for all your friends!

Ancient Egypt
www.ancientegypt.co.uk/life/activity/main.html
An online version of Senet, a board game played by the ancient Egyptians. Players must have Shockwave on their computer in order to play.

APPENDIX C:

PUZZLE SOLUTIONS

There are:

5 Scarab Beetles
5 Pyramids
5 Suns
7 Nile Rivers

CHAPTER 1: WHAT IS A MUMMY?

Death Decay • 2

Orange vegetable = C A R R O T

Thin soup = B R O T H

A slow run = T R O T

Turn around = R O T A T E

Colorful bird = P A R R O T

Past tense of write = W R O T E

Opposite of sister = B R O T H E R

Keep from harm = P R O T E C T

Why Not Rot? • 2

Why didn't Egyptian mummies rot?

The Egyptians worked hard to make sure that we did not!

Dried Out or Frozen • 3

First 2/5 of **MUMMY**	MU
Middle 1/3 of **SUMMER**	MM
Middle 1/2 of **LIFE**	IF
First 2/3 of **ICE**	IC
Last 2/3 of **CAT**	AT
Last 1/2 of **POTION**	ION

Cave Mummies • 3

DRYNESS *and* SALTY MINERALS

112

Water, Water • 4

An adult human body is $\boxed{60}$ % water.

All Sorts of Mummies • 5

N	The suN and warM winds can dry out a corpse.	M
A	Extreme cold will freeze And preserve A body.	A
T	SomeTimes organs were removed, dried, aNd replaced.	N
U	MoistUre can be reMoved from a body using salt.	M
R	FiRe and smoke Are both good drying methods.	A
A	An Acidic, wet environment prevents Decay.	D
L	ChemicaLs can also be used to preserve thE body.	E

The Oldest Mummies • 7

2 Then remove all of the organs.	**7** Finally, add a mask and wig.	**5** Place the skin back on top of the paste.
6 Paint the replaced skin with special minerals that turn black.	**4** Cover stuffed body with white paste made from ashes.	**1** First, take all the skin off of the mummy-to-be.
3 Stuff the empty body with clay, straw, fur, etc.		

A World of Mummies • 6

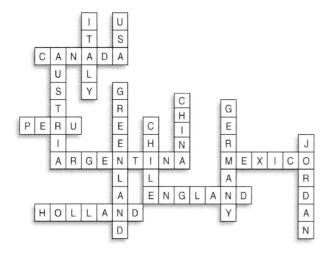

Going Up! • 8

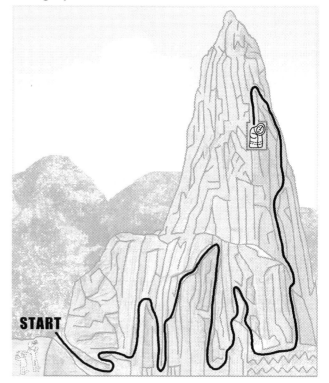

Bog Bodies • 9

1. CCORMIMMOINNALS
   COMMON CRIMINALS

2. PHHAYNSDIICCAALPLPYED
   PHYSICALLY HANDICAPPED

3. HSUAMCARNIFICE
   HUMAN SACRIFICE

Yummy? • 9

WHAT THE MUMMIES LAST ATE!

What's Inside? • 10

MUMMY BUNDLE

Is any body home?

Many Mummies • 11

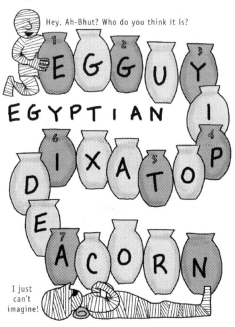

Hey, Ah-Bhut? Who do you think it is?

EGGUYI
EGYPTIAN
DIXATOP
DEA
ACORN

I just can't imagine!

Planning Ahead • 12

T	H	E	█	P	R	O	C	E	S	S	█	T	O	O	K
A	B	O	U	T	█	T	E	N	█	Y	E	A	R	S	,
A	N	D	█	D	I	D	N	'	T	█	A	L	W	A	Y	S
W	O	R	K	█	O	U	T	█	R	I	G	H	T	!	

PUZZLE SOLUTIONS

CHAPTER 2: FAMOUS PHARAOHS

What's in a Name • 14

1A T	2A H	3B E		
4B G	5B R	6C E	7B A	8C T
9C H	10A O	11B U	12C S	13C E

A. Opposite of cold

$\underset{2}{H}\ \underset{10}{O}\ \underset{1}{T}$

B. To fight with loud words

$\underset{7}{A}\ \underset{5}{R}\ \underset{4}{G}\ \underset{11}{U}\ \underset{3}{E}$

C. Bed linen used as a ghost costume

$\underset{12}{S}\ \underset{9}{H}\ \underset{6}{E}\ \underset{13}{E}\ \underset{8}{T}$

Originally the word pharaoh meant the house in which the king lived *(the palace or great house)*, but not the king himself!

Only One • 14

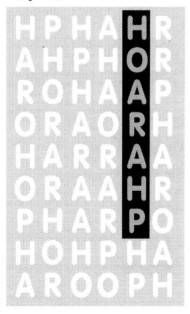

Link to the Gods • 15

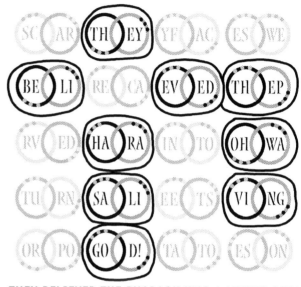

THEY BELIEVED THE PHARAOH WAS A LIVING GOD!

D Is for Divine • 16

HE WORE A FAKE BEARD HELD ONTO HIS CHIN WITH A CORD.

PUZZLE SOLUTIONS

Girls Rule! • 17

S H E   **W O R E**

A   **F A L S E**

B E A R D

How Do I Look? • 17

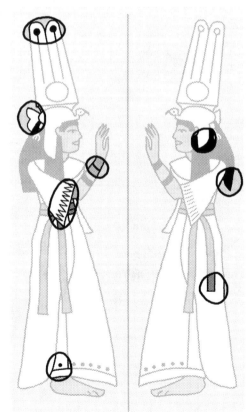

King Tut • 20

1. A T E
2. B A T H
3. B E D
4. C A B
5. D O O R
6. D U T Y
7. F A K E
8. H I D
9. H I N T
10. J U G

Sob! • 20

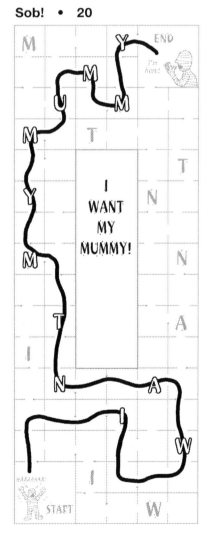

I WANT MY MUMMY!

PUZZLE SOLUTIONS

Pha-ha-ha-raoh • 21

Pizza Tut!
1 2 3 4 5 6 7 8

Drama Queen • 21

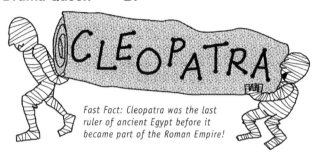

Fast Fact: Cleopatra was the last ruler of ancient Egypt before it became part of the Roman Empire!

Good King at Giza • 22

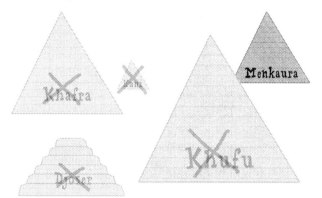

What a Great Guy! • 23

King <u>R A M S E S</u> the second ruled for <u>67</u> years.

Shaking Things Up • 24

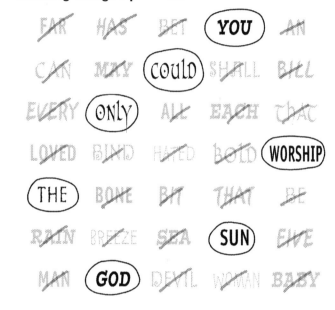

CHAPTER 3: LAND OF MANY GODS

Many Choices • 26

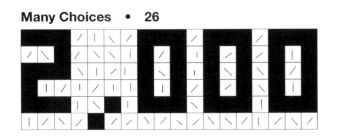

Who Are You? • 26

SIRUNSE — **SUNRISE**
NNOO — **NOON**
TUSESN — **SUNSET**
MNA — **MAN**
RLEDE — **ELDER**
OBY — **BOY**

(SUNRISE—ELDER, NOON—BOY, SUNSET—MAN)

The Big Cheese • 27

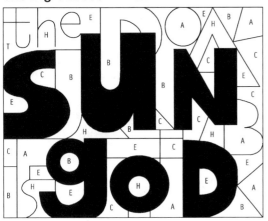

SUN GOD

Hidden Gods • 27

Long a**go d**esert winds swept sand through Egypt.

Two woven baskets hun**g od**dly on the good wall.

The golden pa**god**a had eight gorgeous gongs.

Some car**go d**elivered yesterday was gone today!

Sad God, Glad God • 28

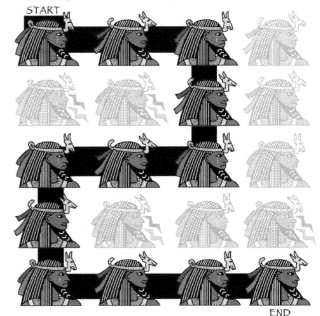

START

END

Busy Beetle • 29

H	E		P	U	S	H	E	D		T	H	E
S	U	N		A	C	R	O	S	S		T	H	E
S	K	Y		E	A	C	H		D	A	Y	.

PUZZLE SOLUTIONS

Yuck • 29

Scarab beetles push around
balls of animal <u>D</u> <u>U</u> <u>N</u> <u>G</u>.

change the U to O = <u>D</u> <u>O</u> <u>N</u> <u>G</u>

change the G to P = <u>D</u> <u>O</u> <u>N</u> <u>P</u>

change the D to P = <u>P</u> <u>O</u> <u>N</u> <u>P</u>

change the N to O = <u>P</u> <u>O</u> <u>O</u> <u>P</u>

Eye of Horus • 32

Above and Below • 33

SHU god of the **AIR**
GEB god of the **EARTH**

Small Protector • 34

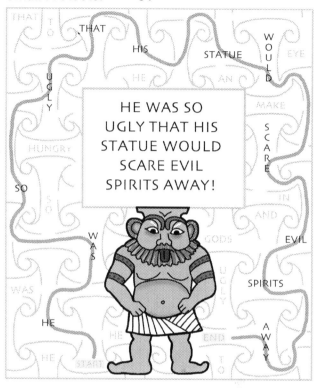

HE WAS SO UGLY THAT HIS STATUE WOULD SCARE EVIL SPIRITS AWAY!

Balancing Act • 35

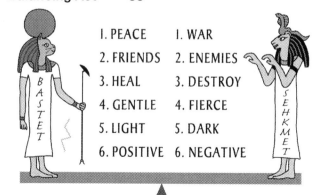

BASTET		SEHKMET
1. PEACE	1. WAR	
2. FRIENDS	2. ENEMIES	
3. HEAL	3. DESTROY	
4. GENTLE	4. FIERCE	
5. LIGHT	5. DARK	
6. POSITIVE	6. NEGATIVE	

PUZZLE SOLUTIONS

Happy Hathor • 35

1. BEAUTY
2. DANCE
3. MUSIC

Before and After • 36

SCARED = **AFRAID**

IN THE MIDDLE = **CENTER**

TO PICK UP = **LIFT**

OPPOSITE OF LIVE = **DIE**

The Egyptians made mummies because they believed in an

A F T E R L I F E

CHAPTER 4: A BUSY AFTERLIFE

~~~~~~

Old Body, New Life • 38

They believed that a person could live again after death — but he needed his whole body for this to happen!

Body Parts • 39

STOMACH   **INTESTINES**   **LUNGS**   **LIVER**

The **BRAIN** was pulled out through the nose with a long hook, while the **HEART** was left in the body.

First Class • 38

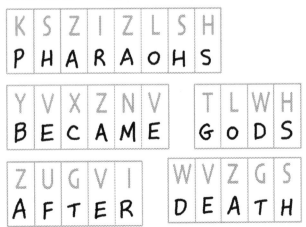

K	S	Z	I	Z	L	S	H
P	H	A	R	A	O	H	S

Y	V	X	Z	N	V		T	L	W	H
B	E	C	A	M	E		G	O	D	S

Z	U	G	V	I		W	V	Z	G	S
A	F	T	E	R		D	E	A	T	H

All Dry • 40

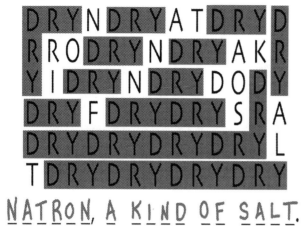

NATRON, A KIND OF SALT.

Say "Aaahh" • 40

"OPENING OF THE MOUTH" was a ceremony that had up to seventy-five different steps!

Mummy Math • 41

A. +8 +4 = 12

B. +29 -10 = 19

C. +15 +5 = 20

D. +10 +9 = 19

TOTAL 70

Ba Humbug! • 42

Good Luck • 43

Where Are You? • 43

BA C KA C H E

BA Z O O KA

BA N KA B L E

Watch Out! • 44

HUNGRY CROCODILES

GIANT SNAKES

EVIL MONSTERS

FIERY FURNACES

Road Map • 44

Weigh In • 45

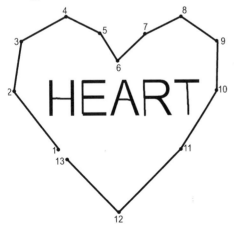

Gulp • 45!

1B A	2A M	3C M	4F U	5C T	
6D W	7A O	8C U	9F L	10E D	
11D S	12B W	13F A	14E L	15D L	16E O	17A W
		18C T	19F H	20B E	
	21D H	22A E	23D A	24B R	25B T	!

Make It "To Go" • 46

PUZZLE SOLUTIONS

Pretty Pictures • 47

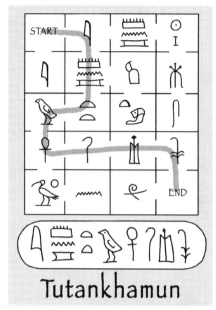

Tutankhamun

Best Buy • 48

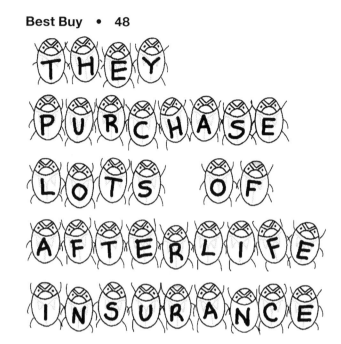

THEY PURCHASE LOTS OF AFTERLIFE INSURANCE

CHAPTER 5: PUZZLING PYRAMIDS

Hide and Seek • 50

Step It Up • 51

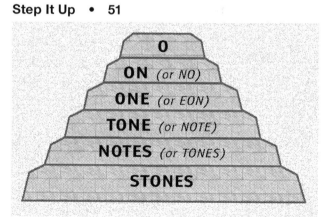

O
ON *(or NO)*
ONE *(or EON)*
TONE *(or NOTE)*
NOTES *(or TONES)*
STONES

PUZZLE SOLUTIONS

Not Just a Builder • 52

IMHOTEP, Chancellor of the King of Lower Egypt,
First after the King of Upper Egypt, Administrator
of the Great Palace, Hereditary Nobleman,
High Priest of Heliopolis, Builder, Chief Carpenter,
Chief Sculptor, and Maker of Vases in Chief.

How Odd! • 52

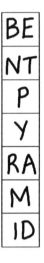

BE
NT
P
Y
RA
M
ID

Float by Boat • 53

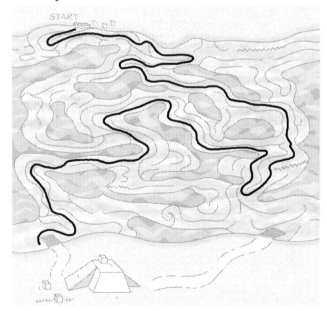

Side by Side • 54

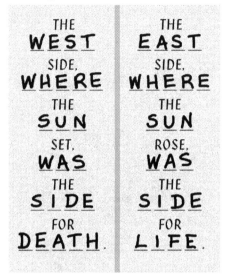

THE **WEST** SIDE, **WHERE** THE **SUN** SET, **WAS** THE **SIDE** FOR **DEATH**.

THE **EAST** SIDE, **WHERE** THE **SUN** ROSE, **WAS** THE **SIDE** FOR **LIFE**.

Tools of the Trade • 55

How High? • 56

The Great Pyramid at Giza is 481 feet tall.

Wonder of Wonders • 56

IT
IS
THE
ONLY
ONE
OF
THE
SEVEN
WONDERS
OF
THE
ANCIENT
WORLD
THAT
STILL
EXISTS!

Hidden Ha Ha • 59

What did one pyramid say to another pyramid?

"How is your mummy?"

People Power • 58

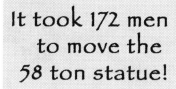

It took 172 men to move the 58 ton statue!

No More Pyramids? • 60

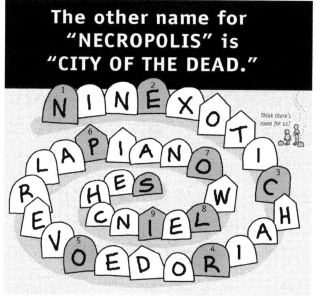

The other name for "NECROPOLIS" is "CITY OF THE DEAD."

PUZZLE SOLUTIONS

CHAPTER 6: TREASURES OF THE TOMBS

Finding Tut's Tomb • 62

This is what Howard Carter said when he first peeked into the tomb by candlelight: "At first I could see nothing...but...as my eyes grew accustomed to the light, details...emerged slowly from the mist, strange animals, statues, and gold - everywhere the glint of gold."

I Spy Treasure • 63

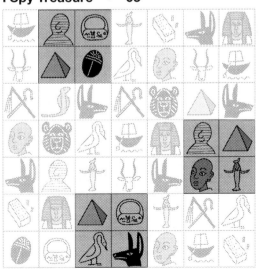

R Is for Royalty • 64

Things that Mr. and Mrs. Pharaoh would recognize: RAINBOW, RAIN, RAYS (of the sun), RAT, RUNG (of the ladder), ROPE, ROOSTER, RABBIT, RUG, RING, RICE, RATTLE, RIBBON.

Things that Mr. and Mrs. Pharaoh would not recognize: RIFLE, ROCKET, RAKE, RACECAR, RECORD PLAYER, RHINO, RULER, RATTLESNAKE, REFRIGERATOR, ROBE, ROLLER SKATES, ROWBOAT, RAILROAD TRACKS, ROBOT, ROCKING CHAIR, RADIO, ROSE, REMOTE CONTROL.

Pet Packages • 65

_F_ DOG
_E_ CAT
_D_ BABOON
_A_ CROCODILE
_C_ RABBIT
_B_ FALCON
_G_ IBIS

Choosing a Coffin • 66

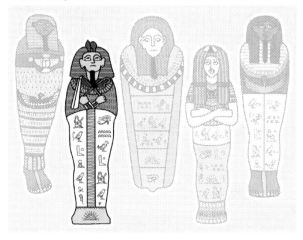

PUZZLE SOLUTIONS

Hieroglyph Sudoku • 67

Precious Past • 68

Black and white
striped animal = Z E B R A

Fruit for cider = A P P L E

Japanese poetry = H A I K U

House of snow = I G L O O

Opposite of sad = H A P P Y

Nut of the oak tree = A C O R N

Liquid that falls as rain = W A T E R

Opposite of below = A B O V E

To frighten = S C A R E

Not easy to bend = S T I F F

Hidden Chamber • 69

Mummy Madness • 70

A. Opposite of over
U N D E R
15 48 18 40 2

B. Kids' stomach
T U M M Y
46 4 7 9 27

C. Young person
C H I L D
50 25 49 34 6

D. A brainstorm
I D E A
32 38 17 13

E. Opposite of out
I N
19 37

F. To speak
S A Y
16 41 11

G. Animal that oinks
P I G
31 43 1

H. Past tense of swing
S W U N G
26 12 8 5 45

I. Person, place, or thing
N O U N
44 3 29 20

J. Kiss
S M O O C H
14 10 22 47 21 39

K. Opposite of push
P U L L
30 23 33 42

L. Green lawn plant
G R A S S
24 28 36 35 51

PUZZLE SOLUTIONS

Just Joking • 71

W	H	A	T		D	I	D		T	H	E		T	O	M	B		R	O	B	B	E	R
S	A	Y		T	O		T	H	E		M	U	M	M	Y		M	A	K	E	R	?
			W	R	A	P		I	T		U	P		A	N	D		I	'	L	L
T	A	K	E		I	T		H	O	M	E		W	I	T	H		M	E	!

Small yet Special • 72

8 hand amulets

1 earring

7 scarabs

4 daggers

6 eye rings

6 slave statues

2 hieroglyph rings

2 crocodile pull-toys

2 hippo statues

2 toy boats

CHAPTER 7: MUMMY FEVER

Hinky Pinkies • 74

What do you call a mummy who...

...is made out of sticky candy?

G U M M Y   M U M M Y

...is very friendly?

C H U M M Y   M U M M Y

...eats crackers in bed?

C R U M B Y   M U M M Y

...is not very smart?

D U M M Y   M U M M Y

What do you call ...

...a mummy's favorite card game?

M U M M Y   R U M M Y

...where a mummy's navel is?

M U M M Y   T U M M Y

Dead and Gone • 75

1. PERISHED
2. DECEASED
3. DEPARTED
4. LIFELESS

Signed Copies • 75

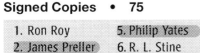

1. Ron Roy
2. James Preller
3. Mary Pope Osborne
4. Kate McMullan
5. Philip Yates
6. R. L. Stine
7. Wendelin Van Draanen

Trick or Treat • 76

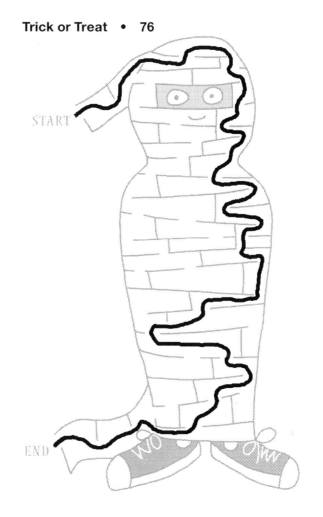

START

END

You're Covered • 76

Kara can wrap up three of her friends.
- There are 12 inches in a foot.
- 5,520 inches divided by 12 = 460 feet of TP needed to wrap one mummy.
- 460 feet divided by 115 (the number of feet in each roll) = 4 rolls of TP needed to wrap one mummy.
- Kara has a dozen (12) rolls of toilet paper; 12 divided by 4 = 3 completed mummies!

Fright Night • 77

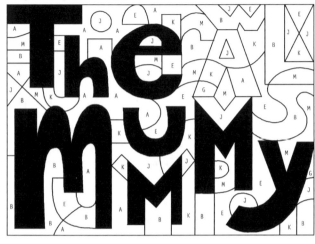

Tons o' Mummies • 78

There are 18 mummies.

Show Offs • 79

The mummy of Ramses II traveled with

HIS OWN PASSPORT

His occupation was listed as
"King (deceased)."

Love My Tunes • 80

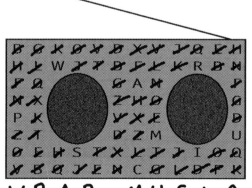

WRAP MUSIC

PUZZLE SOLUTIONS

Take a Dip • 81

THE DEAD SEA

Fun Field Trip • 82

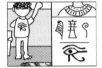
C 2

C 4

A 4

B 1

B 2

A 3

C 1

B 4

C 3

B 3

A 2

A 1

What U Need 2 B • 84

131

PUZZLE SOLUTIONS

Picture Play • 88

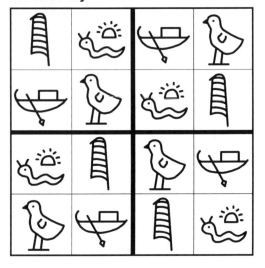

Popular Pyramids • 90

A	F	M	A	U
G	L	A	S	S
E	Y	P	K	E

P	I	A
A	N	D
N	K	D

A	A	R	B	A
S	T	E	E	L
H	E	D	T	L

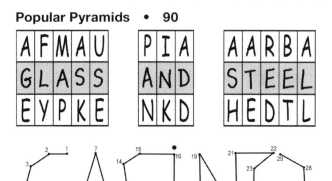

Great Games • 89

Kids in ancient Egypt
played a game called

K H U Z Z A
11 - 8 - 21 - 26 - 26 - 1

L A W I Z Z A
12 - 1 - 23 - 9 - 26 - 26 - 1

Kids today play
a game called

L E A P F R O G
12 - 5 - 1 - 16 - 6 - 18 - 15 - 7

Pyramid Power • 89

O N   T H E   B A C K
O F   A   O N E
D O L L A R   B I L L.

It's a Plan • 91

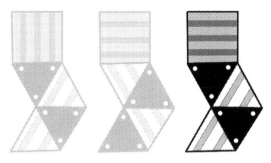

Medicine Man • 92

**CHIEF OF
DENTISTS
AND
PHYSICIANS**

Dr., Dr. • 92

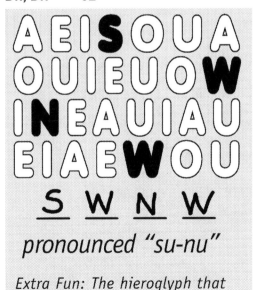

pronounced "su-nu"

_Extra Fun: The hieroglyph that
you see with the puzzle is the
way that ancient Egyptians
would have written this word!_

Wow! • 93

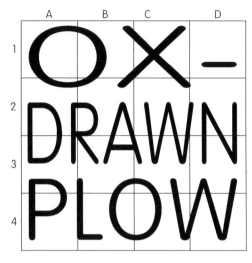

Say What? • 94

Possible Answers: GIRL, GLORY,
GOPHER, GORY, GRIP, GRIPE,
GROPE, HE, HER, HERO, HI, HIGH,
HIP, HIRE, HIS, HOG, HOLIER,
HOLY, IS, LIP, LOG, OGRE, OH, PIE,
PIER, PLIERS, PRY, RELY, RIG, RIP,
RISE, ROLE, ROPE, ROSE, ROSY,
SHE, SHIP, SHIRE, SHORE, SHY,
SIGH, SLEIGH, SLY, SO, SPY.

PUZZLE SOLUTIONS

Money Before Money • 94

There is more than one way to complete this puzzle.
Here is our answer! Was yours the same?

A. GOOSE   B. BIRD   C. FABRIC   D. TOY HORSE   E. NECKLACE
PITCHER   BASKET   BALL   ARROWS
          4 SODAS   4 SODAS
          DOLL

Cool Clothing • 96

CHAPTER 9: HIGH TECH MEETS THE MUMMY

Safely Scientific • 98

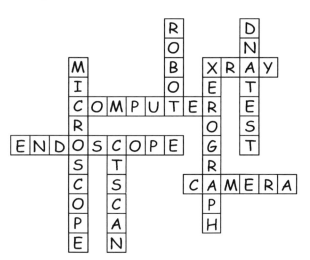

Royal X-ray • 99

THE
ARMS
ARE
CROSSED!

PUZZLE SOLUTIONS

Taking a Peek • 100

To go on forever = ENDL<u>E</u>S<u>S</u>

Light purple = <u>L</u> <u>A</u>VENDE <u>R</u>

Warm and pleasant = <u>F R I</u> E <u>N</u>D<u>L</u>Y

Machine to mix food = <u>B</u> <u>L</u> E N <u>D</u> <u>E</u> <u>R</u>

Positive ID • 101

	TRUE	FALSE
The weather in Egypt is cold.	R	(D)
Pharoahs were kings.	(N)	O
Egyptians worshipped many gods.	(A)	P
Amulets were worn for bad luck.	S	(T)
A pyramid could be built in a year.	U	(E)
King Tut's tomb held many treasures.	(S)	C
A sarcophagus was a stone coffin.	(T)	N
Making a mummy took 3 days.	E	(I)
There is a pyramid on a US dollar.	(N)	L
It was an easy journey to the Afterlife.	D	(G)

<u>D</u> <u>N</u> <u>A</u> <u>T</u> <u>E</u> <u>S</u> <u>T</u> <u>I</u> <u>N</u> <u>G</u>

DNA is our unique genetic code. Although every person's DNA is different, some parts of your DNA pattern are the same as other members of your family. DNA testing can prove whether or not a group of mummies are related!

What a Nose • 102!

To decode the message, choose the letter one row down and one key to the right of each letter shown on the computer screen.

....

HIS NASAL CAVITY
WAS STUFFED WITH
PEPPERCORNS!

Modern Mummies? • 104

In the process called **<u>PLASTINATION</u>**, water and fat in the body are replaced by...

First 3/4 of PLAY = <u>P</u> <u>L</u> <u>A</u>

Last 1/2 of MOST = <u>S</u> <u>T</u>

Second 1/4 of FIND = <u>I</u>

First 1/3 of COW = <u>C</u>

In the process called **<u>CRYONICS</u>**, the body is preserved by...

First 2/3 of FRY = <u>F</u> <u>R</u>

Middle 1/2 of NEED = <u>E</u> <u>E</u>

First 1/4 of ZERO = <u>Z</u>

Middle 1/2 of MIND = <u>I</u> <u>N</u>

Last 1/5 of CLANG = <u>G</u>

PUZZLE SOLUTIONS

Go, Rover! • 105

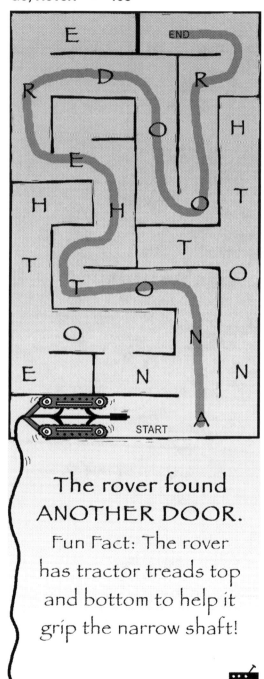

The rover found ANOTHER DOOR.

Fun Fact: The rover has tractor treads top and bottom to help it grip the narrow shaft!

Cause of Death • 105

1. APPLE
2. BRAG
3. COLD
4. DEAD
5. DOWN
6. DRIP
7. FLAME
8. GATE
9. GHOST
10. HORN
11. JOLLY
12. LOST
13. MAGIC
14. NICE
15. PASS
16. RATE

To understand what these scientists do, all you need to do is look at both parts of this word. "Paleo" means "very old". A "pathologist" is someone who studies the effect of diseases.

Close Encounters • 106

1. **HAND**
2. **SKULL**
3. **TEETH**
4. **KNEES**
5. **FOOT**
6. **SHOULDER**
7. **NECK**
8. **CHEST/RIBS**

PUZZLE SOLUTIONS

Closed for Repair • 107

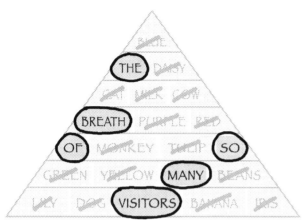

Dead End • 108

Look Again! • 109

1. Dried Out or Frozen

2. D Is for Divine

3. Balancing Act

4. Ba Humbug!

5. No More Pyramids?

6. Finding Tut's Tomb

7. Fun Field Trip

8. Money Before Money

9. Dead End

Printed in the United States
By Bookmasters